# Crowdfunding and Crowdsourcing in Journalism

This book offers an in-depth exploration of crowdfunding and crowdsourcing in journalism today, and examines their impacts on the broader media landscape.

*Crowdfunding and Crowdsourcing in Journalism* looks at how these practices disrupt traditional journalism models, including shifting journalistic norms, professional identity, and the ethical issues at play when journalists turn to social media and the Internet to solicit widespread support. While there is often a lot of hype and hope invested in these practices, this book takes a critical look at the labour involved in crowdsourcing journalism practices, and the evolving relationship between audiences and journalists, including issues of civility in online spaces. The author draws on in-depth interviews with journalists in Canada and the United States, as well as examples from the United Kingdom, Germany, Sweden, and Australia, to provide a comprehensive study of increasingly important journalist practices.

The book is a valuable resource for academics, researchers, and journalists who are interested in political economy, journalism studies, and labour studies.

**Andrea Hunter** is an Associate Professor in the Department of Journalism at Concordia University. She is the Director of the Concordia Centre for Broadcasting and Journalism Studies.

T0347541

# Disruptions: Studies in Digital Journalism
Series editor: Bob Franklin

**Disruptions** refers to the radical changes provoked by the affordances of digital technologies that occur at a pace and on a scale that disrupts settled understandings and traditional ways of creating value, interacting and communicating both socially and professionally. The consequences for digital journalism involve far reaching changes to business models, professional practices, roles, ethics, products and even challenges to the accepted definitions and understandings of journalism. For Digital Journalism Studies, the field of academic inquiry which explores and examines digital journalism, disruption results in paradigmatic and tectonic shifts in scholarly concerns. It prompts reconsideration of research methods, theoretical analyses and responses (oppositional and consensual) to such changes, which have been described as being akin to 'a moment of mind-blowing uncertainty'.

Routledge's new book series, *Disruptions: Studies in Digital Journalism*, seeks to capture, examine and analyse these moments of exciting and explosive professional and scholarly innovation which characterize developments in the day-to-day practice of journalism in an age of digital media, and which are articulated in the newly emerging academic discipline of Digital Journalism Studies.

**Crowdfunding and Crowdsourcing in Journalism**
*Andrea Hunter*

**Digital Innovations and the Production of Local Content in Community Radio**
*Josephine F. Coleman*

**Participatory Journalism in Africa**
*Hayes Mawindi Mabweazara and Admire Mare*

For more information, please visit: www.routledge.com/Disruptions/book-series/DISRUPTDIGJOUR

# Crowdfunding and Crowdsourcing in Journalism

**Andrea Hunter**

LONDON AND NEW YORK

First published 2021
by Routledge
2 Park Square, Milton Park, Abingdon, Oxon OX14 4RN

and by Routledge
52 Vanderbilt Avenue, New York, NY 10017

*Routledge is an imprint of the Taylor & Francis Group, an informa business*

*British Library Cataloguing-in-Publication Data*
A catalogue record for this book is available from the British Library

*Library of Congress Cataloging-in-Publication Data*
A catalog record has been requested for this book

ISBN: 978-0-367-36068-9 (hbk)
ISBN: 978-0-367-74691-9 (pbk)
ISBN: 978-0-429-34363-6 (ebk)

Typeset in Times New Roman
by Taylor & Francis Books

# Contents

# Acknowledgements

First, my thanks to the journalists who I interviewed as part of this research. Their insight and experience was vital to the making of this book. I am grateful they took time out of their busy lives to talk to me. The work they are doing is inspiring.

Parts of this book were written through periods of pandemic lockdown that slowed things down at times. My thanks to the editor of this series, Bob Franklin, whose encouragement and support of this project was vital to seeing it through.

Thanks also to Priscille Biehlmann and Jennifer Vennall at Routledge for their guidance.

Finally, thanks to my family for their unwavering support and sense of humour.

Research funding for this project was provided by the Social Sciences and Humanities Research Council of Canada.

The subsection 'Crowdfunding' in Chapter 1 and the sections of Chapter 2 that focus on crowdfunding draw in part on work that first appeared in: Hunter, A. (2016). "It's like having a second full-time job": Crowdfunding, journalism and labour. *Journalism Practice, 10* (2), 217–232. Sections of Chapter 3 that focus on crowdfunding first appeared in: Hunter, A. (2015). Crowdfunding independent and freelance journalism: Negotiating journalistic norms of autonomy and objectivity. *New Media & Society, 17*(2), 272–288.

# 1 Change and continuity

Over five weeks during the spring of 2013, two Dutch journalists, Rob Wijnberg and Ernst Pfauth, raised just over $1.7 million (USD) through crowdfunding. Their goal was to start an independent online journalism platform called *De Correspondent*, which would offer something different from mainstream media. As Pfauth put it, *De Correspondent* is a place where readers can find "background, analysis, investigative reporting, and the kinds of stories that tend to escape the radar of mainstream media because they do not conform to what is normally understood to be 'news'" (Pfauth, 2013, para 1). Almost 19,000 Dutch people donated money, at least $80 each, to make it happen. That same year, across the Atlantic Ocean, in Toronto, Canada, freelance journalist Naheed Mustafa crowdfunded just over $15,000 (CAD) to support a reporting trip to Pakistan and Afghanistan. As Mustafa described in her pitch, her goal was to "write and produce several stories about how conflict and war have changed the lives of people in the region" (Mustafa, 2013, para 1). It was a much smaller amount than *De Correspondent*, but still significant for Mustafa as it allowed her to offset her freelancing costs and do the kind of in-depth reporting she hoped would be much more impactful than what she'd been able to produce before. It would give her the ability to slow down a bit, not worry about quantity, and focus on quality.

> [T]o offset the costs for these types of overseas projects, I have to churn out an incredible volume of work. Most of what I produce on these reporting trips is simply for the purpose of paying my way. I end up with very little time to invest in the types of deeper stories that require patient, focused reporting and lots and lots of time – the kind of stories that give readers and listeners a better understanding of the reality in the region.
>
> (Mustafa, 2013, para 15)

These are just two examples of a multitude of both small and large crowdfunding ventures that journalists and would-be journalists have undertaken in recent years. As Pfauth and Mustafa did, many of them are taking this on because they want to offer something different than what they see in legacy media. Through crowdfunding, harnessing the power of the Internet to reach potential donors, they are trying to change the landscape of journalism.

Similarly, crowdsourcing, where journalists appeal to audiences through the Internet for story ideas, sources, and expertise, is also changing how journalism is conducted/produced and what it looks like. For example, in 2017 ProPublica and National Public Radio (NPR) in the United States launched a project they called "lost mothers." Their aim was to investigate deaths and near-death experiences related to pregnancy and childbirth in the United States. They had the statistics that each year between 700 to 900 women die during pregnancy or due to complications related to childbirth. They also knew that "for each woman who dies, more than 70 nearly die" (Gallardo, 2018, para 1). They also had a few names of some potential sources they'd gathered from maternal health professionals. But although this was a good start, they needed more.

> [W]e still didn't have enough of the human stories we needed for this project. So we set out to find women and families willing to share intimate experiences. To do that, we published a request: Do you know someone who died or nearly died in childbirth? Help us investigate.
>
> (Gallardo, 2018, para 2)

The help came quickly. Within days 2,500 people had responded, which quickly grew to nearly 5,000 responses from all 50 states. In the end, with readers' help, they were able to tell a harrowing series of stories documenting serious failings in the US maternal health system, including the stories of 134 women who had died during childbirth (NPR, n.d.; ProPublica, n.d.).

This was a large-scale crowdsourcing exercise, but crowdsourcing is also used daily by journalists trying to connect quickly with sources outside their personal connections. In March 2020, for instance, when the Covid-19 pandemic had just started to hit Canada, some universities were making quick decisions to close their campuses, move classes online, and empty out residences. Christopher Curtis, a reporter with the *Montreal Gazette*, was writing a story on deadline and wanted to speak to students who were being asked to leave their residences. He put out a call on Twitter and within hours had connected with sources that might otherwise have been hard to find, the interviews got done, and the story was out on deadline.

Crowdfunding is sometimes characterized as a form of crowdsourcing, but this book will distinguish between the two: crowdfunding means going to the crowd for financial support, while crowdsourcing involves going to the crowd for help with journalistic content, such as sources, expertise, fact-checking, and even sorting through data. Both are often positioned as empowering for journalists. Crowdfunding gives journalists a chance to create work outside legacy media's walls, thanks to donors who are willing to help fund new media ventures or support a journalist's freelance reporting. Crowdsourcing opens up new avenues for story-telling, easy access to a wide array of potential sources and experts. In addition to being empowering for journalists, crowdfunding has also been heralded as a way to create a more "participatory" type of media environment in which the "former audience" (Gillmor, 2004) takes on a more active role. Instead of sitting back and passively consuming journalism, they get to participate in the creation of journalism by financially backing projects they believe in. A recent Pew Research Center report spoke glowingly of the potential of crowdfunding to support "a new niche segment of non-traditional journalism driven in large part by public interest and motivation," and bring "voice and visibility to efforts that would likely otherwise go unnoticed or unfunded" (Vogt & Mitchell, 2016, para 10). Similarly, crowdsourcing has also been championed as a way to open up journalism, or democratize the media, by involving more people as sources, fact-checkers, and even as part of investigative pieces, including participating in data-driven journalism (Aitamurto, 2016; Bradshaw & Brightwell, 2012; Lowrey & Hou, 2018).

However, beyond this hype and the discourse of opportunity, there are some serious issues at play as crowdfunding and crowdsourcing become more common in journalism. This book explores how traditional journalism models are disrupted by these practices, including labour practices, journalistic norms, professional identity, and the ethical issues that arise when journalists turn to social media and the Internet to solicit widespread support—both for finance and for content. It also examines the evolving relationship between audiences and journalists in crowdfunding and crowdsourcing, including issues of civility in online spaces. Much of the focus is on the labour and ethical implications of crowdfunding, particularly what happens when the imagined "wall" between business and journalism collapses. As journalists and would-be journalists negotiate their relationships with funders, they have to grapple with how much influence funders have, or should have, over the content they produce. As well, not only is crowdfunding very labour-intensive to the point where it is prohibitive for many, it requires a set of entrepreneurial skills that can be at odds with journalists who see themselves as public servants. This can mean a profound shift in professional identity for those who are not already comfortable with marketing or the world of business in general. This book will also address how journalists who crowdfund are negotiating ideas around journalistic norms, such as "fair and balanced" or "objective" approaches to reporting. Although the idea of objectivity in reporting has often been critiqued as either impossible or undesirable (Calcutt & Hammond, 2011; Lowery, 2020; Maras, 2013; Tuchman, 1972; Winston & Winston, 2021), or a misunderstood concept that should not be equated simplistically with neutrality or balance (Rosenteil, 2020a, 2020b, 2020c, 2020d, 2020e, 2020f), it is still a norm that guides much legacy media (Deuze, 2011; Gasher, Skinner, & Lorimer, 2020; Winston & Winston, 2021). Some journalists who crowdfund say they strive to adhere to these ideals, but many others are turning to crowdfunding precisely because they want to create advocacy journalism or what I have called journalism with a "point of view"—journalists who believe they can report accurately and truthfully, while maintaining a distinct position. Although much of the focus of this book will be on journalists and the work they do, this book will also examine the role of donors in crowdfunding, arguing that we should think of what donors do as work, and situate their labour within concepts of the audience commodity (Smythe, 1981).

As with crowdfunding, this book will also consider the labour issues involved in crowdsourcing, the ethical challenges that occur when inviting the "crowd" into the journalistic process, and how this type of participatory journalism affects journalists' sense of professional identity. Crowdsourcing, by its very nature, forces journalists to be more open and transparent about the work they are doing, a practice that flies in the face of traditional ways of reporting, particularly investigative reporting where journalists are used to keeping story ideas under wraps for fear of being scooped. Like crowdfunding, it can also be very labour-intensive and require active participation on social media, which isn't always easy to step away from and take a break. Crowdsourcing requires journalists to think about the boundaries they need to set up online and how much of themselves they are willing to put "out there." The "crowd" is also working in crowdsourcing, contributing their time and energy, whether it's through an interview or actively sorting through data.

This book draws on interviews with 50 journalists who have crowdfunded and/or participated in other types of crowdsourcing. The interviews were conducted between 2013 and 2020. Most of these journalists work in Canada or the United States, with the exception of one who worked in France. The majority of journalists who participated in these interviews are not identified, as anonymous interviews allowed them to speak openly and honestly about their work without potentially jeopardizing their employment or business.[1] I also draw on crowdfunding campaigns found on crowdfunding-specific platforms such as Kickstarter and Indiegogo, websites of individual media organizations that are crowdfunding as part of their overall business plan, crowdsourcing social media posts on Twitter, and news sites where journalists are reaching out to audiences to crowdsource different material.

The purpose of this book is to map out the complex web of crowdfunding and crowdsourcing models that are currently used in journalism through the use of illustrative examples and best practices that are being developed. But while this book may give some guidance for those interested in crowdfunding and crowdsourcing themselves, it is not built as a how-to. Rather, the goal is to cast a critical eye on practices that are often suffused with powerful pro-entrepreneurial or pro-technological rhetoric that tends to ignore or downplay the realities of labour, ethical issues, and disruptions to professional journalistic norms that need to be examined thoughtfully. While I share the belief with many journalists in this book that crowdfunding and crowdsourcing can be powerful tools that help tell stories that might otherwise go untold, I am also wary of offloading the responsibility of financing journalism onto individual journalists or small journalistic organizations. I am similarly concerned about the labour implications of these practices, including the extra responsibilities put on journalists who feel obliged to add crowdsourcing to their daily work schedule. Finally, I hope this book adds to the conversation already underway about shifting journalistic norms or "boundaries" (Carlson & Lewis, 2015) as journalists and journalism educators consider both the continuities and disruptions these new practices bring to our work. Instead of adopting new practices quickly just because at first glance they seem to offer possibilities that will only make the profession that much better, we need to consider what journalistic norms (if any) should remain foundational, what needs to shift and how we can define the work we do with these new tools. My hope is that this book gives the reader a sense of how journalists who crowdfund and crowdsource are grappling with these ideas.

## Book structure

This chapter continues with an overview of how crowdfunding and crowdsourcing have been used in journalism to date, including some of the most prevalent models for these practices that are currently in use. Chapter 2 will focus on labour issues. As mentioned, crowdfunding can be an enormous amount of work. A successful crowdfunding campaign isn't a "build it and they will come" type of situation, rather it requires sustained outreach and follow-up with donors. This can be so time-consuming on platforms like Kickstarter that one journalist described it as a "second full-time job" ($47,500 USD, Kickstarter). Similarly, crowdsourcing can require building and sustaining relationships with a wide array of people, which can be very time-consuming. As well, both crowdfunding and crowdsourcing require a type of labour that can seem very different for journalists, whether it's adopting business practices or being transparent about your work. This chapter also considers the work of the "crowd," and how audiences are implicated in these practices. Chapter 3 examines how the journalistic norms of autonomy and independence are invoked in crowdfunding and crowdsourcing. This includes how journalists interpret these ideas in the context of any responsibility they may feel towards their funders and the people who are helping them crowdsource stories. This chapter also looks at how the journalistic norms of verification and accuracy are translated in crowdsourcing, including how transparency is used when verification becomes impossible. Chapter 4 explores the ways journalists are using crowdfunding and crowdsourcing to report on stories they don't see in legacy media, or bring a diverse range of sources and ideas into the news-making process. The chapter situates the work of journalists within the sociological theory of structuration, that asks us to think about the larger societal structures we all work and live under, and the agency that individuals may or may not have within these structures. This chapter provides examples of how journalists are trying to open up journalism, either by creating venues for stories that may not find a home in legacy media, or widen the range of sources they use. Finally, Chapter 5's focus will be on best practices, and it will look at how crowdfunding and crowdsourcing are working to redefine and reinforce the boundaries of journalism as a profession and practice.

## Crowdfunding

Since the 2008 recession, jobs in legacy media in North America have become increasingly scarce as journalism organizations struggle to remain financially viable (Grieco, Summida, & Fedeli, 2018; McChesney & Pickard, 2011; Public Policy Forum, 2017). Around the world there are similar stories to tell (Nel, 2010; O'Donnell, Zion, & Sherwood, 2016; Viererbl & Koch, 2019). More recently, the economic shutdown due to Covid-19 has also taken a toll, with some predicting that the impact may be even greater than the 2008 downturn (Silverman, 2020). As journalism organizations lose advertising revenue, we've seen some ask their staff to take pay cuts, cancellations of paid internships, as well as a multitude of layoffs and closures (Cox, 2020; Donnelly, 2020; Silverman, 2020). It is within this context of job losses and closures that crowdfunding has been heralded as one way for struggling journalists or would-be journalists to fund their work, either by bolstering their freelance budgets or creating new online platforms for their work (Aitamurto, 2011, 2015; Carvajal, García-Avilés, & González, 2012; Hunter, 2015, 2016; Hunter & Di Bartolomeo, 2018; Jian & Usher, 2014; Porlezza & Splendore, 2016).

Much of the early hype and hope around crowdfunding came from some high-profile cases where journalists were raising far more than they asked for, in some cases by hundreds of thousands of dollars (Hunter, 2015). One of the earliest success stories was *Matter*—a science and technology magazine that raised $140,000 (USD) on Kickstarter. While this might not seem like much in comparison to crowdfunding campaigns for video games that have raised millions (Parker, 2017), for journalism this was phenomenal, especially since they had originally asked for one-third of that amount. Why were they so successful? There were three reasons. First, the *Matter* campaign was launched by two journalists who already had impressive credentials. Jim Giles' work had been published in *Nature, The Atlantic, The Economist*, and *New Scientist*. Bobbie Johnson had been a technology columnist for the *Guardian* and had also undertaken work for the BBC and the *New York Times*. Second, it didn't hurt that they had some famous friends from the tech start-up world who were willing to appear in their Kickstarter promotional video—Alexis Ohanian from Reddit, Cory Doctorow from the website Boing Boing, Matt Haughey who founded Metafilter. But the crux of their success was a pitch that appealed directly to their audience's intelligence and desire to support smart, independent journalism. While they did offer rewards in exchange for donations, such as t-shirts, books, and invitations to launches, the campaign really focused on the idea that people should support them financially because they would be funding independent, serious journalism that would contribute to making the world a better place. *Matter* was pitched as an antidote to the frivolity and ignorance that exists on the Internet when it comes to science and tech reporting, something an intelligent reader (and of course potential donor) would (and should) want. They began their pitch by spelling out the "problem" they were trying to deal with:

The web is the future of journalism, but let's be honest: the future isn't living up to expectations. Newspapers and magazines have cut back on in-depth reporting. Gossip sites have proliferated. The web has become a byword for fast and cheap. Why isn't it synonymous with fearless, investigative, and enthralling writing? We think it can be.

(Johnson, 2012, para 3)

They went on to outline how they were going to create "independent, global, in-depth reporting about science and technology," a magazine that would be "the new home for the best journalism about the future" (Johnson, 2012, para 5). To do this, they would "need you to help us make it happen" (Johnson, 2012, para 5).

*Matter* was the first to create big waves, but very quickly there were others which followed. In a similarly high-profile and successful campaign that same year a former NPR journalist raised over $100,000 (USD) on Kickstarter to start an independent publication to cover Washington politics (Seabrook, 2013). A couple of years later, the collective Radiotopia raised over $600,000 (USD) on Kickstarter to fund independent podcasts (PRX, 2015). But along with these big success stories there are a plethora of more modest examples; journalists raising anywhere from a few thousand to tens of thousands of dollars. Many journalists are trying, as *Matter* was, to raise money to create their own independent online magazines or independent documentaries. They're turning to crowdfunding because funding is not easy to come by for new media ventures, and this is a way to solicit start-up funds, and keep their publications going. As one journalist said, they would not have been able to launch a publication on their own because "it's way too expensive" and securing a loan was not a viable option as banks do not look kindly on new media ventures ($11,700 USD, Kickstarter). Others are crowdfunding to support their freelancing, trying to raise enough funds to do reporting which they then hope to sell to legacy media. For freelancers in particular, crowdfunding has been touted as one way to support their work in a financial climate where freelance budgets of legacy media organizations are drying up or simply non-existent (Carvajal, García-Avilés, & González, 2012). As one freelance journalist who regularly contributes to legacy media said, most of the venues she usually works for have disappeared. "Either the shows had been cancelled or the budgets for the shows had shrunk so ridiculously that they simply couldn't afford to pay for anything" ($16,000 CAD, Indiegogo). Faced with this reality, crowdfunding allowed her to pay for travel and expenses upfront, without having to worry right away about selling a story.

Another journalist says he now uses a hybrid model to finance his freelance journalism—he gets some funds from legacy media, but also raises funds through crowdfunding to cover his expenses so that he can be guaranteed to make some money.

> They'll [legacy media] pay me for a piece but it costs me $5,000, $6,000 to get on a plane and stay in a hotel for weeks, hire a fixer and do all the things that journalists need to do, it costs a lot of money. If I'm getting $500–1,000 for a piece it's just not going to add up to enough money to cover all my travel expenses and pay my mortgage and health insurance and food and everything else. So what crowdfunding does, is it covers my travel expenses and some extra so that I am guaranteed to make some money before I even write anything.
>
> ($33,200 USD, Kickstarter)

Another freelance journalist said she was finding it hard to get her "foot in the door" ($1,600 USD, Spot.us). Editors wouldn't take her pitches seriously because she did not have much of a portfolio so she used crowdfunding to raise enough money to produce stories on her own that she could then sell as finished products.

Then there are larger organizations, such as ProPublica in the United States, *The Tyee* in Canada, and the *Guardian* in the UK that use crowdfunding as one part of their overall business plans. Often the call for crowdfunded support is couched in the idea that independent journalism is a cornerstone of a functioning democracy. At the bottom of most *Guardian* stories, for instance, there is a small text box asking readers to donate. While the wording can change from story to story, the underlying message remains the same: your donation will help keep their reporting autonomous, and allow them to pursue investigative and explanatory journalism that is vital to a healthy society.

## Crowdfunding models

At its core, crowdfunding simply means what the name suggests—going to the "crowd" to solicit funding for something. Usually the fundraising is dispersed, with a multitude of people making small donations (Bannerman, 2013; Belleflamme, Lambert, & Schwienbacher, 2014; Mollick, 2014). It can seem rather unwieldy when looking at the range of crowdfunding that exists today, but generally there are four types of crowdfunding models that can be distinguished based on what donors get in return: equity, lending, rewards, and donation (Aitamurto, 2015;

Bannerman, 2013; Hunter, 2015, 2016; Mollick, 2014). In an equity-based model, investors donate with the expectation that they are now part of the project, and will share in the profits. In lending-based models, investors expect their money back, with interest. These two models are really aimed at attracting investors who want to put their money into something that will give them a financial return.

The models typically used in journalism, donation- and rewards-based, get away from this idea of investment. In the donation-based model contributors give altruistically, without expectation of compensation of any sort. News organizations, such as the *Guardian*, that ask for reader support can be seen as fitting into this model. Their content is freely available online, whether you donate or not. This is different from a subscriber model that news organizations like the *New York Times* use, where people pay to have access to content. In a rewards-based model, crowdfunding campaigns are built on a tier system where there is the promise of a tangible "reward" based on how much a person donates. Two of the most common rewards-based platforms used by journalists are Kickstarter and Indiegogo. Kickstarter is an all-or-nothing platform, meaning that you have to raise all the money you ask for (or more) to collect the funds, but if you don't raise your goal you don't get anything. According to Kickstarter, the reasoning is this assures the money will be there to create what's been pitched and donors' investments will result in something tangible (Kickstarter, n.d.b). On Indiegogo, by contrast, you can collect whatever you raise, even if you don't meet your goal. When people donate on these rewards-based sites, the rewards are usually minimal for small donations, but become more substantial the more a person donates. Coming up with rewards can be fairly straightforward if you are crowdfunding for a creative project that has a tangible, known outcome, like a video game or a movie. One of the most well-known examples of this type of crowdfunding was for the Veronica Mars movie. Veronica Mars was originally a "teen noir" TV series that ran for just three seasons in the mid-2000s starring Kirsten Bell as a sardonic, misunderstood high-school private eye. It gained such huge cult following that when it was cancelled and the series creator turned to Kickstarter to see if fans would finance a movie, it became the platform's most-backed campaign of all time as of 2014. Thomas wanted to raise just over $2 million (USD), but ended up making $5.7 million (John, 2014). For small donations people received copies of the script ($10) or t-shirts ($25). For bigger donations the stakes were higher, signed copies of posters or invitations to the premiere. Then there were the big-ticket items. If you had $800 to spend, you could name a character. A $10,000 donation got you a speaking role (Thomas, 2013). Journalism, however, does not fit into this model as easily as a movie. How do you market rewards when (a) you may not be sure what you are going to produce (every journalist knows stories can end up very different from the original plan) and/or (b) you are creating something you may want to give away for free as a public good? As will be detailed in Chapter 2, in the face of these realities, journalists have had to be creative.

Aitamurto (2011) has identified four different categories, or reasons, journalists crowdfund that are tied to the type of work they are trying to produce. First, there are journalists who are crowdfunding to solicit money to cover one particular story. Freelancers, for instance, will turn to crowdfunding to cover their reporting costs in order to increase their odds of making a profit when they sell their work. The second category is made up of journalists who are fundraising to cover a certain beat they feel is underreported. Elly Blue, from Portland, Oregon in the United States, for instance, has run multiple crowdfunding campaigns on Kickstarter to create magazines focused on feminist bicycle culture, a topic she's passionate about, but which doesn't get a lot of attention in mainstream media (Blue, 2012). Then there are journalists who are raising seed money to start their own online news ventures. Usually they're doing this because they see a hole in the media landscape. For example, independent journalists Mariève Paradis and Sarah Poulin-Chartrand from Montreal, Quebec in Canada raised just over $11,500 (CAD) on Kickstarter to start an online magazine to cover parenting issues in French. Canada is a country with two official languages, English and French, with French spoken most predominantly in the province of Quebec. They called the magazine *Planète F* (F for famille), which translates in English to "Family Planet." In their pitch, they explained that they saw a big hole in the French parenting media market in their province. Most parenting magazines were full of what they considered fluff reporting: ideas for crafting projects, product reviews, and the like. In short, not a lot of serious reporting. They wanted to change this. In *Planète F* they promised that readers would not find "cupcake recipes" or "Hallowe'en costume ideas," instead the focus would be on "in-depth reporting" and "intelligent debates" to do with family and health (Paradis & Poulin-Chartrand, 2014, para 30). The final category is made up of journalists who are fundraising to support something adjacent to the actual journalism content they are producing. An example of this would be the San Francisco Public Press, an independent investigative journalism organization that raised over $20,000 (USD) on Kickstarter so their newspaper could be delivered by bicycle (Hunter, 2016).

What these categories miss, however, is that crowdfunding is also being integrated as one part of a larger business plan with news organizations, not just for start-up funds, but rather as an integral part of a news platform's financial survival. Sometimes crowdfunding is targeted towards a specific project, such as ProPublica's efforts to investigate the "intern economy" that examined whether interns were being fairly paid for their labour (McDermott, 2013). In other instances, crowdfunding is just one part of the general fundraising efforts. *The Tyee*, an online Canadian news outlet that focuses its reporting on issues that affect the West Coast province of British Columbia, gets one-third of its funding from crowdfunding. The rest comes from philanthropic support as well as some advertising. As they explain on their website, they rely on crowdfunding, which they call "reader support," to keep "articles free and open for everyone to read" (Tyee, n.d., para 4). They add that reader support also lets them pay their writers "fairly" and "stay completely focused on publishing truly valuable journalism for our readers, instead of being driven to sell advertising" (Tyee, n.d., para 4). *The Tyee*'s reader support should not be confused with subscriptions as their content is freely available, unlike a subscription or membership model where information is behind a paywall that you can only access by subscribing.

## Crowdsourcing

Crowdfunding can be seen as a specific type of crowdsourcing that is part of a larger movement in journalism to draw on the crowd to create work. Onuoha, Pinder, and Schaffer (2015) describe crowdsourcing in journalism as "the act of specifically inviting a group of people to participate in a reporting task—such as newsgathering, data collection, or analysis— through a targeted, open call for input; personal experiences; documents; or other contributions" (para 4). Within this definition, they identify two sorts of crowdsourcing. The first is an unstructured call-out, where journalists generally encourage people to contact them with information or story ideas through email, phone calls, or social media. The second is a structured call-out where people are asked to respond to a specific question or complete a specific task. Whether it's structured or unstructured, they argue that "crowdsourcing requires a specific call-out" (para 8). As they write: "If a newsroom simply harvests information or content available on the social web, we don't believe this constitutes crowdsourcing. For us, the people engaging in crowdsourcing need to feel they have agency in contributing to a news story" (para 8). This idea of agency is an important one that will be dealt with in the next chapter that considers the labour of people who contribute to news stories. Participating in the news process is often painted very altruistically, as an opportunity for audiences to participate in a profession that plays an important part in a democracy. However, not to be forgotten in these ideas of agency and opportunity, is the nagging question of labour. There is work that happens here. The next chapter will look at what exactly this work entails and who it benefits.

That said, this book takes the position that journalists who find information on social media and then use it in a news story *are* crowdsourcing, as there are ways this can happen where the "crowd" plays an important, even vital, role. For instance, when a tornado touched down in the province of Saskatchewan, Canada on July 4, 2020, local resident Craig Hilts posted a picture of the twister on Instagram, a beautiful, yet terrifying shot from a dirt road. The image consisted of a field, with far-off buildings, and the funnel cloud clearly reaching down to touch the ground in the distance. The tag read: "Tornado on the ground south of Glenbain, Saskatchewan 4:30 pm" (Hilts, 2020). Within 45 minutes, journalists were posting on his account asking if they could use the photo on the news, to which he answered yes, but to please give him credit. The picture showed up on several newscasts and online stories. In this case, Hilts wasn't responding to a call-out, but clearly became part of the news process, a witness to an event who provided valuable visuals that brought a new dimension to the story. Similarly, when news organizations go to content on Twitter to find out what is happening during breaking news events, such as a protest or a natural disaster like an earthquake, when there aren't reporters on the scene, it is also a form of crowdsourcing—a conscious use of material from the "crowd" to paint a fuller picture of a news event. It is also a form of crowdsourcing when journalists mine social media for ideas and sources, and then use what they find to construct their stories. Matt D'Amours, a journalist with the Canadian Broadcasting Corporation (CBC), described crowdfunding from the point of view of the journalist as either active or passive. For him, active crowdfunding involves "looking for posts on social media and actively reaching out to somebody who has posted." As he put it:

> I do think this is a form of crowdsourcing because you're looking on social media for somebody, or a form of content, or a discussion about a given topic. I can't tell you how many news stories began with "hey, I saw this tweet" or "hey, I saw this Facebook post" and then you reach out to that person.

He described a general call-out on Twitter or other social media as passive crowdfunding, as it doesn't start with an active search for sources and information. Either way, whether it's initiated by a direct call-out, or initiated by the journalist who finds information on the Internet and then reaches out to sources, the "crowd" becomes implicated in the story, helping to bring it to "life".

## Crowdsourcing models

There are generally six typologies of crowdsourcing, which are tied specifically to what audiences are being asked to do (Onuoha, Pinder, & Schaffer, 2015). The first is voting, where audiences are asked to prioritize the stories that journalists should be chasing. As an example, WBEZ Chicago, an NPR radio station and website, often asks audience members to let them know what stories they want investigated and then asks people to vote. The station describes what they are doing as becoming more transparent about the news process and involving the crowd in editorial decision-making. They call it an "ongoing news experiment" and that by including the public in this way they are going to "make journalism more transparent and strengthen multimedia coverage about Chicago, the surrounding region and its people (past or present)" (WBEZ, n.d., para 1). Perhaps not surprisingly, some of the recent stories they've looked into have to do with Covid-19, such as safety tips on eating in restaurants as restrictions relax and how to get tested for the virus (Eng, 2020a, 2020b). The second type is witnessing, where audiences are asked to share what they saw as a news event unfolded. This is often used in crisis reporting when journalists are looking for first-hand witnesses to events such as earthquakes, hurricanes, or protests, where there aren't journalists on the scene or when they're looking for diverse perspectives. The third is asking audiences to share their personal experiences, as in the "lost mothers" story crowdsourced by ProPublica and NPR. The fourth category is tapping into specialized expertise where audiences are asked to contribute information or specific knowledge they might have to a story. This could be tapping into people's everyday experience, such as a newspaper in Sweden, *Svenska Dagbladet*, that wanted to look into how mortgage rates differed across the country and asked readers to submit information from their area (Aitamurto, 2016). Or it could mean asking for people with specialized knowledge to contribute their expertise to a story. Some crowdsourcing call-outs combine calls for expertise with personal experience. For instance, ProPublica has been looking for people with expertise and/or stories about being affected by Covid-19.

This type of call-out lies somewhere between the structured and unstructured call-out. While there is definitely a topic they are interested in, their call for help is wide-ranging.

> Are you a public health worker or front-line medical provider? Do you work for or with a government agency involved in the effort to protect the public? Have you or your family personally been affected? Show us what we should be covering, or serve as an expert to make sure we're on track.
>
> (Allen et al., 2020, para 2)

The fifth type of crowdsourcing is when the audience is asked to complete a task, volunteering their time or skills to help build stories, such as when the *Guardian* created a database of MP expenses and asked readers to help them go through it. As the *Guardian* explained when they launched the project: "This is an enormous potential dataset, comprising four years' worth of expenses and claims outlining MPs' mortgages, second home purchases, duck houses and soft furnishings" (*Guardian*, 2009, para 2). They wanted the public's help to go through the information they'd uploaded, over 170,000 documents, to see if they could uncover any interesting and important stories. They were hoping to build a picture over time of how MPs' expenses have changed. As another example, ProPublica asked readers to forward them any correspondence they'd received from members of government about the future of a federal law that aimed to make health care insurance more affordable for Americans. ProPublica had already fact-checked an email sent from a Senator to a constituent that they found to be "misleading" and lacking "important context" (Parris, 2017), and they wanted to expand their investigation. The organization asked readers to "email their member of Congress and tell us what they say" (Tobin et al., 2019, para 4). Finally, the last category of crowdsourcing is "engaging audiences", where journalists reach out to interact with audiences around lighter or more "playful" topics (Onuoha, Pinder, & Schaffer, 2015). For instance, asking people to submit funny stories or pictures of their pets, or asking them to vote on their favourite food or restaurants.

## Crowdsourcing and crowdfunding pre-Internet

In October 2012 Hurricane Sandy hit the eastern seaboard of the United States where it made landfall as a Category 2 storm. It was a devastating hurricane, leaving over 70 people dead in the United States and over 70 billion (USD) in damages (CNN, 2020). When the storm settled, donations were quick to stream in to the US Red Cross for the clean-up and recovery. The response was overwhelmingly generous, but a year and a half later there were lingering questions about where the money had gone. In April 2014 ProPublica published a story wondering how the $312 million was spent, and asking anyone with information to reach out (Elliot & Eisinger, 2014). Editor-in-Chief Stephen Engelberg said the story was "unusual" for them in that it "focused on what we could not figure out" (Engelberg, 2014, para 9). Over the next few months they sifted through tips that came in from people working for the Red Cross, former employees and others who had inside knowledge. Thanks to these people who offered their inside information and expertise, the two reporters, Justin Elliot and Jesse Eisinger, were able to team up with NPR to produce a story that detailed where the money went and where it didn't (Elliot, Eisinger, & Sullivan, 2014), including "a devastating internal report in which the Red Cross acknowledged botching the post-Sandy relief effort and diverting assets 'for public relations purposes'" (Engelberg, 2014, para 11). As Engelberg pointed out after the story was published, this type of reporting—asking readers for help and input on a story—has existed long before the Internet. As an example, he pointed to William Safire, a *New York Times* columnist, who "used to throw sly references into his stories to entice cooperation from the handful of government officials who had his phone number. He called it 'putting a note on the bulletin board'" (Engelberg, 2014, para 12). The difference today, as Engelberg rightly points outs, "is that this board is much larger and more easily shared with vast numbers of people. All you've got to do is ask the right question in the right way" (Engelberg, 2014, para 13).

While the remainder of this book focuses on the disruptions that occur when journalists crowdfund and crowdsource, it is important to remember there is continuity that exists. Journalists have always relied on the "crowd" to help them tell stories. In fact, new journalists are encouraged from the beginning to cultivate a wide circle of friends and acquaintances, the idea being that the wider your social circle, the more chances you'll have of happening upon stories. Stories don't only come from "official" sources or news releases; stories are all around you and some of the best can come from your friends or acquaintances. News outlets have also routinely encouraged people to call, email, and write letters with story ideas, or contribute to their programming by sharing their personal experiences or expertise. For example, the Canadian Broadcasting Corporation has regular noon-hour radio shows across the country that rely on listeners calling in to share their experiences or opinions about the topic of the day, or ask questions to guests on the show. Similarly, every Sunday afternoon there is a program called *Cross Country Checkup*, where listeners call in with questions for the guests of the day or to tell their own stories about whatever the topic happens to be. Subjects can range from serious issues in the news, such as slowing the spread of Covid-19, to lighter issues, such as what people are reading during the summer.

Although crowdfunding today is shorthand for online fundraising, crowdfunding is not exclusive to the Internet (Bannerman, 2013; Jian & Usher, 2014). It has been common practice for public broadcasters in North America to ask audiences for monetary support. For NPR and the Public Broadcasting Service in the United States, the tradition of yearly fundraising campaigns where listeners and viewers are asked to pledge their support goes back decades. In Canada community radio stations also have a strong tradition of yearly fundraising campaigns.

With these continuities in mind, the rest of this book focuses on the differences and the disruptions that occur when these practices move online. While crowdfunding and crowdsourcing through the Internet open up opportunities for journalists, there are significant challenges. While crowdfunding online makes it easier for individual journalists who do not have large institutional support to connect directly with potential funders (Hunter, 2015; Jian & Shin, 2015), it also forces journalists to act as entrepreneurs, a type of work they may not be used to and can seem at odds with journalism. While it opens up opportunities for new sources of funding, it also changes the relationships news organizations and journalists have with their audiences who are now donors, and raises questions about accountability and ethics. Similarly, online crowdsourcing offers opportunities, allowing journalists to tap into a wide array of sources and solicit help from audiences, whether it's helping sort through data or contributing valuable insight and expertise. But at the same time crowdsourcing also changes the way journalists work, as they must become more transparent about the stories they are investigating and spend time cultivating online connections. While crowdfunding can be liberating, it can also be constraining. The next chapter examines the labour involved in crowdfunding and crowdsourcing, particularly the time it takes to use them effectively and how it changes the nature of work.

## Note

1  The interviews were conducted over the phone, Skype, or Zoom. The interviews were semi-structured in that journalists were asked about their motivation for crowdfunding and/or crowdsourcing and how they found the experience, but the interviews followed the path the journalists took and the points they

wanted to raise. For the journalists who crowdfunded, I have identified how much they raised to give the reader a sense of how large their projects were. Many of these crowdfunding journalists were not currently employed by a legacy news media outlet, but were either crowdfunding to start their own news sites or freelancing. If applicable, I identify whether they had previously worked in legacy media, including freelancing. For the "would-be journalists," people who were crowdfunding in order to start their own news sites or begin their freelancing careers, I simply identify them as journalists and give details about why they were crowdfunding. For journalists who are currently working at established legacy news organizations and talked to me about crowdsourcing, I do not identify what news outlets they work for, as part of the premise of participating in this research was that they could speak on condition of anonymity and that their employer would not be named. What I have done is identified whether they are early-career, mid-career, or senior journalists to give the reader a sense of their experience level.

# 2 Labour

## Introduction

Crowdfunding has been touted as something journalists can turn to when money is tight and jobs are scarce, the suggestion being that when faced with an uncertain job market becoming an entrepreneur is perhaps the best or only option (Zara, 2013). While cautioning that crowdfunding is not a replacement for legacy business models, Aitamurto (2015) still sees crowdfunding as playing "an important role in the emerging new business model ecosystem in journalism" (p. 203), not just because it can help journalists raise money, but because crowdfunding is also a marketing tool that can help journalists brand themselves, test story ideas, and attract audiences. Similarly, crowdsourcing is also positioned as a practice that is empowering for journalists, fostering new opportunities to reach out to audiences for story ideas, expertise, and even help in sifting through data to create stories. Crowdsourcing means engaging audiences, finding new stories to tell, and diversifying the news ecosystem. Much of the hype around this idea of agency and power is about changing journalism from a top-down "lecture" into a conversation between journalists and audiences who are no longer being "told" the news, but helping shape it (Onuoha, Pinder, & Schaffer, 2015).

However, what is often overlooked amidst the hope and possibility is the amount and the type of labour involved. When journalists are running campaigns on crowdfunding-specific platforms like Kickstarter or Indiegogo it can be extremely time-consuming and exhausting, to the point where it can feel like journalists have a second full-time job. It is also a type of entrepreneurial work that forces journalists to act in ways they may not be accustomed to or comfortable with. Most journalists are used to pitching their ideas "in-house" to editors or producers, but having to become entrepreneurs and sell an idea to potential funders before they can even begin the work of reporting is something different. It can be difficult to be publicly transparent about their story ideas before they have been fully formed and produced, let alone having to market their work and justify why it's worthy of funding. Similarly, crowdsourcing can also be very labour-intensive and requires journalists to be transparent about their work in a way they may not be used to. Particularly for investigative journalists who are used to keeping a story under wraps until it's time to publish so they're not scooped, being open about your work from the beginning is a very different way of operating.

While much of this chapter will examine labour from the journalist's perspective, it will also consider the work that donors and audiences are taking on. Crowdfunding and crowdsourcing are also often positioned as empowering for audiences. In crowdfunding donors are able to back work they find interesting and important, helping it come to "life." In crowdsourcing audiences have a chance to participate in news creation through their own experiences or expertise. But, using Dallas Smythe's (1981) concept of the audience commodity, this chapter also asks the reader to consider how the audience is "commodified" through crowdfunding, essentially *becoming* the product, rather than simply *supporting* a product. This chapter also involves the reader considering that audiences who participate in crowdsourcing are essentially working for free, donating their time, stories, and expertise to help create journalism. While this could be framed as an opportunity for people to participate in an important part of democracy, it is still a form of labour that needs to be considered when taking a wide lens approach to how journalism is constructed. As well, it asks the reader to consider how both journalists and audiences are "prosumer commodities" (Fuchs, 2012) when they use social media to facilitate or participate in crowdsourcing and, moreover, that by using social media, audiences are essentially working for these platforms, filling them up with content and, in turn, their information is being sold to advertisers.

## Crowdfunding: it's like having a second full-time job

To put it bluntly, crowdfunding on platforms such as Kickstarter or Indiegogo, where you have one month to raise the money you need, is a lot of work. First, there is the planning stage, where thought and strategizing need to go into designing and writing the pitch, thinking about how best to refine and sell your ideas to potential donors. But no matter how beautifully written, it is not enough to simply put up text about what you want to achieve. It has become standard practice, and recommended, to produce compelling video, pictures, and graphics

(Condon, 2017). Many journalists said that the work involved in the design is so intense and requires such a diverse skill set, that it's difficult for one person to do this alone. But while it helps to be part of a team, even then it can be overwhelming. For example, one journalist who was raising money to start an online magazine said her campaign was successful because she was working with people who had professional writing and design skills, but even though they had a good team together and could spread the responsibilities around it was "still a ton of work … It was completely insane. I would never do it again" ($76,000 USD, Kickstarter).

Designing a campaign also means thinking about the system of rewards that will entice people to donate. When crowdfunding for a creative product such as a movie or a game, there are fairly obvious rewards to go to—the marketing material that goes along with the product, such as t-shirts, hats, or buttons, or there is the product itself. With journalism, coming up with rewards is more difficult. It can be hard to offer a "product" as a reward. Journalists who are crowdfunding to cover a single story, particularly an investigative story, are not always sure what the end product will even be. Journalists who are crowdfunding to start an online publication often want their publication to be open to anyone, freely available on the web, so the "product" can't be offered as something exclusive. Given these realities, journalists have had to think creatively. Some freelance journalists who were raising funds to travel would offer postcards or trinkets from the places they were travelling to. Some journalists decided to offer exclusive content, behind-the-scenes details, or advance copies of their work. For the highest donations, some journalists would even offer to go for dinner or drinks with donors. However, because many found it difficult to think about tangible rewards that would be big draws, they often decided the best strategy was to focus on appealing to a person's interest in the story or the publication itself. For example, one journalist who ran a campaign to fund a feminist online publication said she eventually decided it was best to focus on appealing to a donor's desire to see a women's magazine that did not focus on celebrity content. She said there were other people running crowdfunding campaigns for feminist magazines who had a lot of connections and were able to offer what she called "big ticket" rewards, such as a consultation with a writer for a well-known television programme. But since she didn't have these types of contacts, she had to think differently about what she could offer:

> Of course the rewards are really one of the best ways to bring people in to back your projects. So that was something I really had to sit down and think about. For me ultimately it was—OK, well I

don't really have the ability to offer these big ticket items necessarily, so I'm going to focus on offering exclusive or early access to our content and more fun rewards that are sort of related to [magazine]. But it also made me realize maybe my rewards aren't my main draw. I really need to focus on getting people behind [magazine's] mission in general and having that being our selling point.

($15,000 USD, Kickstarter)

Essentially, the journalists who decided to target a donor's sense of altruism, focused on the idea that by contributing funders would be part of something bigger than themselves—that by funding journalism they were really becoming part of the democratic process and bringing to light stories that were not getting coverage in legacy media.

But while there is a lot of work involved in designing a campaign, it is during the month of the campaign itself where the labour becomes really intensive. For a campaign to work, journalists have to do extensive outreach. Social media, Twitter and Facebook particularly, is used to reach out to their networks, advertise their campaigns, and provide updates. They also used their personal contacts to email potential donors individually or even meet people in person. A great deal of time was spent thanking donors and providing updates, in the hopes that people will make a second donation once they see that the campaign is progressing. All the journalists I spoke to said you have to stay plugged into social media for the month of the campaign to keep up the outreach. In short, it is not enough to simply build a site and expect people to find it. As one journalist raising money for an online magazine observed—you cannot send one message out and think it is enough, the process of social media outreach is really about building relationships with donors and this takes time.

You have to have a solid plan for outreach. That's building partnerships, which is a lot of phone calls, a lot of emails, a lot of meetings, a lot of research and contacting people who would be interested. Social media. It's a lot of work.

($1,600 USD, Spot.us)

Similarly, one journalist said for herself and her partner, the month of the crowdfunding campaign was about getting their names and their idea out to potential funders, rather than sitting back and watching the money come in. As she described: "The month of the campaign was really a marketing campaign more than just a money campaign. We knew we had to email people and be on Facebook and be on Twitter" (journalist, $11,600 CAD, Kickstarter). Another journalist who was raising money to start an online magazine even said that outreach is so important she thinks it is essential to have a social media expert working as part of a campaign:

> A good tip would be to have someone in your pocket who knows about social media and how to promote it. Because you can write the best copy, and have the best video but if you don't have a way to promote it and get people to see it, it's not going to go any-where. It's not going to be successful.
>
> ($30,500 USD, Kickstarter)

Most journalists described the crowdfunding campaign as exhausting. As this journalist described, crowdfunding to start an online magazine at the same time that he was working his regular jobs was overwhelming. "It nearly killed me to make it happen. On top of running the site and the other jobs I do because I don't get paid enough by [current employer], it was an extraordinary effort" ($20,000 USD, Indiegogo). Similarly, another journalist who raised money to start a news site described the process as stressful as well as extremely time-consuming. "It is exhausting. The campaign itself, from the time you hit go to the time it closes is like having an extra full-time job for a month. It's constant plugging and pushing" ($47,500 USD, Kickstarter).

Many journalists said they were very surprised by the amount of work it took to stay on top of the social media outreach. They had been drawn to crowdfunding after hearing success stories, and cautioned that these stories belie the amount of effort these campaigns take. As this journalist who raised money for an online magazine described:

> I think what's happened with crowdsourced funding is people are hearing about the big stories—the movies that get made, the Planet Money NPR project which raised $500,000 to do a t-shirt. Podcasts that have raised $100,000. What they don't tell you is those people are very, very lucky. Doing a crowdfunded project takes a lot of work and a lot of personal outreach.
>
> ($10,500 USD, Kickstarter)

Several journalists who used Kickstarter as a platform also said that the key to their success was being put on the front page, singled out by the company as an interesting project worth supporting. This brought a lot of visibility to their campaigns, and attracted donors who were outside their social networks. One journalist who had run a successful campaign on Kickstarter to start an online publication as well as an unsuccessful campaign, said that this type of recognition was crucial:

> At the beginning [my successful crowdfunding campaign] wasn't doing terribly well, so [Kickstarter] put it on their front page because they liked the project. Once it was on the front page then it took off. But as long as it was just counting on my own supporters it wasn't doing well enough. It would have failed. You could tell because when they took it off the front page it stopped doing well. Then they put it back on and it made its goal. So, I think that's kind of a secret—the support of Kickstarter itself is really crucial to certain projects. I didn't get that the second time around. They didn't put me on the front page the second time around.
>
> ($25,000 USD, Kickstarter)

Most journalists also said that another crucial aspect of their successful campaigns was reaching out to specific audiences. One journalist, who only raised one-third of the funds she asked for on Indiegogo to support her freelancing, said that if she were to do this again, she would run a more "targeted" campaign:

> In retrospect—this is kind of dumb of me—but I didn't really think about who would actually want to support something like this. What kind of people would have a vested interest in a project like this? If I were to do it again, I would think about it more in that way.
>
> ($1,500 USD, Indiegogo)

She described the way she approached her campaign as "trial and error," and feels that if she had concentrated on approaching people interested in her general topic area—in her case international human rights—she might have been better off.

That said, despite the enormous amount of work, there are some people who run campaigns several times and actually find the process exhilarating. They don't have issues with the marketing aspect of crowdfunding. As one journalist, who has run multiple campaigns to create small magazines, said, she doesn't mind the "hustle" that goes along with crowdfunding, including the publicity that needs to go into it, but she could also understand why some would get burnt out ($48,000 USD, Kickstarter).

While the pace of work is different when crowdfunding is part of an ongoing operation rather than a one-month campaign, there are similar issues at play. Often larger organizations will have positions devoted to audience outreach to mitigate the workload, and business plans need to be designed that differ from the usual advertising-based model. Similar to one-off crowdfunding campaigns, marketing to donors often involves a system of rewards. Sometimes it's small tokens. Sometimes it's exclusive content. At *The Tyee*, for example, readers who pledge their support will get pins, mugs, or tote bags depending on how much they donate. Canadaland, a news and podcasting site in Canada that is funded in part by audience support, offers its donors perks such as ad-free podcasts.

### Crowdfunding: "it's like walking outdoors naked"

In addition to being a lot of work, crowdfunding is also a type of work that many journalists who use crowdfunding platforms are not comfortable with. As mentioned, larger organizations where crowdfunding is one part of a larger business plan often have positions devoted to publicity, outreach, and funding. But for journalists using crowdfunding platforms who are used to dealing with content alone and working at arm's length from the advertising side of journalism, the business aspect of crowdfunding was difficult to deal with. There was a small number of journalists I spoke to who had experience with marketing and did not feel the same reservations as others, but most journalists did not see themselves primarily as entrepreneurs. The process of having to market themselves and ask for donations made them uncomfortable and, at times, felt akin to begging. In short, it can be difficult to embrace the often-conflicting values of public affairs journalism and business.

Journalists who have worked for legacy media organizations are used to having to pitch ideas to producers and editors. The *Washington Post*'s TikTok that parodied reporters pitching to their editors as if they were on an episode of *The Voice*, an American television show where amateur singers compete for the judge's approval, was exaggerated, but also funny to journalists because it wasn't too far off the mark (Jorgenson, 2020). It can be stressful pitching your ideas to editors and producers. While you don't have to wait for a judge to press a button and swivel their chair around to signal your story pitch has been given the green light, you do have to go through an intense process where your ideas are critiqued and examined from different perspectives. This can be an intimidating experience. However, there is some comfort that comes from pitching within a group of colleagues who likely have similar values and a common understanding of how journalism works. Having to pitch your idea to a public of strangers and convince them to fund your work? This is something very different. As one journalist who was crowdfunding in order to freelance described, she felt very uncomfortable being so transparent about her ideas. It did not come naturally and she had to wrestle with the notion that her idea, that she felt was interesting and important, might be rejected or critiqued in a public way:

> It was really uncomfortable at the beginning. I've never been through a public process where you put your idea out there, very publicly in front of everybody that you care about socially and professionally to be rejected. You feel a sense of that every day until it's funded.
>
> ($3,200 USD, Kickstarter)

Similarly, another journalist who had worked in legacy media said having to be open and transparent about an idea before a project was even fully formed was foreign to her. She was used to pitching stories to editors and producers, but doing this in an open format was "scary":

> You're opening the door to the public before you even start reporting and you're having to show proof of concept first. Those are conversations that are often held behind closed doors with just the editor or just a small team of people at the news organization. Then you go out and do the reporting and put it out in the world. That, at least, has been my experience doing big projects. So this was the first time I was really saying—"Here's an idea we have."
>
> ($7,000 USD, Kickstarter)

However, this journalist also said there were some positive outcomes from working this way. She got a lot of helpful feedback on her idea and having to defend her ideas publicly helped her articulate her story more clearly. Through the feedback, she was also able to find more sources for her story. Similarly, another journalist said that although he was not used to "having to justify what you're doing in a very public way," one positive aspect of crowdfunding was that it forced him to be more open and transparent about this process, which is a direction he was hoping to move in anyway (journalist, $19,400 USD, Spot.us).

But despite these positive spins, for the journalists who did not have experience in marketing, overwhelmingly the whole process of asking for money made them uncomfortable, at the very least. One journalist even said it felt almost inappropriate. She had worked for legacy media for almost two decades where she never had to worry about the financial aspect of the business. Crowdfunding to support a new freelancing career made her feel very exposed and vulnerable. Not only was she transitioning into a profession that can be very precarious (Cohen, 2016) and requires new skills to do with managing finances, she found that asking for financial support in a very public way was difficult. As she described, it took some time for her to get used to the idea:

> I had great reservations at first. I tell my friends it felt like walking outdoors naked. Because you're putting yourself out there asking for money and it just felt like walking out in the open, unprotected in a way. Would people think this was inappropriate or not?
>
> ($4,500 USD, Kickstarter)

Another journalist was very blunt. Although he had been very successful at crowdfunding to create an online publication, it is not something he wants to do ever again:

> I hate social media and begging for money. It makes me kind of ashamed to hustle … It makes me feel uncomfortable. I feel like if people don't want to fund me they don't want to fund me and I don't want to be out shaking my cup on the street. It's degrading. It's humiliating.
>
> ($26,000 USD, Kickstarter)

As mentioned, some journalists dealt with this by including people in their campaigns who had a background in fundraising. One journalist who raised money to start an online magazine said they had to expand their team because the process of asking for money can be very difficult for people who come from a strict journalism background. "I think it's one of those things that can be scary for most journalists" ($76,000 USD, Kickstarter).

## Crowdsourcing work

Similarly, crowdsourcing can also be labour-intensive and require journalists to work in ways they may not be used to. In the planning stage, especially with larger crowdsourcing projects, there are many steps that need to be taken into consideration, including how to structure the call-out, who you are going to be targeting, how responses will be collected, and how you will connect and engage with the people who are contributing (Onuoha, Pinder, & Schaffer, 2015). When journalists from the Australian Broadcasting Corporation launched an investigation into the state of long-term care homes in the country, they spent a great deal of time deciding what approach to take and what exactly they were going to ask for—a general call for personal stories or were they trying to get more specific data? In the end, they decided to combine the two strategies, taking a "staggered approach" where they first issued a general call-out asking "residents, family and staff to identify issues they had come across in their nursing homes" (Puccini, Prior, & Filali, 2018, para 40). They would then use this information to help guide their decision-making, chase specific stories, and focus their next call-outs. The next challenge was to figure out the best way to reach people. They decided on a survey and hired a professional researcher to help design the questions. They also had a dedicated email address for people who would rather write to them. The next challenge was getting the word out. They used tactics you might expect, advertising the survey in their own media outlets, but they also hired someone to help get the survey out to communities who might be interested, but wouldn't necessarily see the call-out in the media. Their planning paid off and the initial response was overwhelming—4,000 people answered the call. It was then that they realized the work was just beginning. They would need extra hands to help them sort through the data, as well as a plan to respond to everyone. To keep their respondents up to date on the progression of stories they created a newsletter, which they also used to ask more questions of the audience as needed (Puccini, Prior, & Filali, 2018).

Of course, for a small-scale crowdfunding effort, such as a quick call-out on Twitter to find a source for your story, the planning doesn't have to be as labour-intensive. The challenge with smaller call-outs is getting the "right" question quickly. Something snappy, to the point, that will get responses. In the end, it may not be any more labour-intensive than reaching out to personal networks by email or phone to connect with someone. One journalist who freelances for legacy media said she actually finds it less labour-intensive to respond to people on Twitter than she does through email, and will often use the "like" button to respond, just as an acknowledgement, but doesn't feel pressure to write a big response, as she might with an email that she sees as a more formal mode of communication that requires a thought-out response. But if the response is large, which it potentially can be on a social network, it can take longer to sort through responses. Some journalists also feel an obligation to respond to every person who reaches out. One mid-career journalist said he tries to respond to everyone who answers his call-outs, even if he is not going to interview them for the story he's chasing. First, just out of "common decency," it's courteous to answer people who take the time to reach out. But second, "from a professional standpoint it makes sense to not leave people hanging," in case they may be a useful source for a story he's chasing at another time. This journalist often joins Facebook groups from different communities and says he considers it a "privilege" to be allowed in. Most people are in the group because of a common interest, while he is there looking for stories and he is very cognizant of this difference. He doesn't want to abuse this privilege, so tries to make sure he is respectful by responding when he can. Another early-career journalist said that sometimes she gets so many responses to her call-outs that when she's working on deadline, it's just not possible to answer everyone. As she described:

> It is so much work, especially when I bring it up to the three major platforms—Twitter, Facebook, Instagram. Once I bring it there I'm getting a myriad of different responses and I'm pretty much hyped up on adrenaline trying to get the story done, so I'm just seeing what catches my eye and if it's over a hundred responses it's way too much to say "OK, thank you or OK, next time", kind of thing.

She said she feels very grateful and thankful to the people who respond to her calls, but the reality of working to deadline simply makes connecting with each person an impossibility. "(If) I'm on deadline, I don't have time to respond. I filter through who's going to work best for me."

To crowdsource successfully, some journalists made the point that it is necessary to be on social media regularly to foster community and connections with the people who follow you. One mid-career journalist said he is successful at crowdsourcing because he has created a community online and that needs to be nurtured. He is "very rarely" able to step away from his social media feeds. Even when he went on vacation recently, he said he was "not able to check out." He described it as a vacation that wasn't really a vacation. "I was doing fun things, but I was still very much at work. And that's a problem. That's really hard on your morale." However, he feels an obligation to keep up with people who reach out to him on social media, as they come to him with their difficult stories and put their trust in him to investigate. "They've given a lot of themselves to me. They've taken risks. They've put themselves in a dangerous position. I feel as though it's my responsibility to them to be available."

Crowdsourcing is also a type of labour that journalists may not be used to, as it forces them to be transparent about their work and the stories they are chasing. Traditionally journalists are used to keeping the stories they're investigating under wraps until they're ready to "break." As the Australian journalists who worked on the crowdsourced story into long-term care homes put it:

> Investigative journalists usually like to work in the dark. Like speleologists, they find the first crack into a story, explore the underground, dig in and keep digging until they can finally shine a light on the darkest corners. Their work is often shrouded in secrecy and kept behind closed doors until it's time to publish.
>
> (Puccini, Prior, & Filali, 2018, paras 1–3)

However, some journalists who use social media as part of their investigative tool-kit, make the argument that things are changing, and being open about the story you're chasing can work to a journalist's advantage. As Ken Armstrong, a journalist who works at ProPublica, wrote on Twitter:

> For so long, the conventional wisdom in investigative reporting was: Don't let the world know what you're working on until you publish. But as @propublica's engagement team has shown—thru one powerhouse story after another—that convention needed some serious rethinking.
>
> (Armstrong, 2020)

Sarah Kliff, an investigative journalist at the *New York Times*, responded to Armstrong's tweet, agreeing that being open about an investigation can help with reporting and signal the story is yours:

> Totally agree with Ken on this – this kind of proactive outreach is such a useful reporting tool. And it can work to your benefit: when you let the world know what you're working on, it puts a stake in the ground.
>
> (Kliff, 2020)

That said, for other journalists, old habits are still the best habits. As one mid-career journalist put it, crowdsourcing works well "when you're in a rush to turn around a story that requires really specific access or a really specific perspective," but "it doesn't work for a story when you don't want someone to know you're investigating something." Another mid-career journalist, who works a daily news cycle, but also does some investigative work, agreed, saying he doesn't use public crowdsourcing for investigative work. He doesn't see the value of letting other journalists know what he's working on, and for him it makes more sense to keep your story under wraps until it's time to go public so he doesn't get scooped. Another early-career journalist who also works in daily news said she would prefer not to let her colleagues know what she's up to for fear of being scooped, but it's standard practice and even encouraged at the outlet she works for to post regular updates to social media on stories she's chasing:

> Even when I have had a scoop in the past, I use a clip of what that story is and I tease it out (on social media) because I want people to tune in. I'm using social media as a reinforcement. It's pretty much transparent for the world to know about and we're encouraged to do that.

Some journalists made the interesting point that what helps them investigate is not necessarily being open about the story they're chasing, but being open about themselves. One mid-career journalist said his investigative journalism is helped by being honest on social media about who he is, including his "misgivings and mistakes." As he put it, "my big scoops are more because someone trusts me," and being authentic on social media is one way to build trust. He described himself as being "very vulnerable and open and honest on Twitter" and building an online persona that is very close to his offline persona. "I think the me that I put out there is very close to the 'me' me. The non-performative me." He said being transparent helps his followers feel comfortable coming to him with sensitive information that he's used to break important stories.

## The work of the crowd: the audience as commodity and prosumer

Crowdfunding and crowdsourcing are often positioned as giving audiences agency and power, some measure of control over how journalism works and the stories that are told (Aitamurto, 2011; Porlezza & Splendore, 2016). However, what this overlooks is that audiences are also contributing something important to these processes that needs to be counted when we are considering how journalism gets made—their labour. With crowdfunding, the idea that the audience is working might seem like a bit of a stretch at first glance. How is voluntarily opening your wallet to fund journalism work? And besides, clicking a few buttons to transfer funds from your account to someone else's hardly constitutes heavy lifting. However, some journalists are using crowdfunding as one step towards an advertising model, using their donors as proof to advertisers that they have an audience. For instance, journalists who are crowdfunding seed money for online publications are typically hoping to build up a community of donors, whose loyalty will then translate into advertising dollars. It's a one-time endeavour that they hope will propel them into more sustainable funding through advertising.

> I have a bit of money to really get the site going and get content up there. I'm hoping that that will draw even more viewers and build even more of a community. Then at that point I can use those views to sell sponsorships.
>
> ($15,000 USD, Kickstarter)

Similarly, another journalist said she ultimately wants to raise money for her publication by finding an investor. She wants to grow her publication and says this is not something she can do through crowdfunding campaigns. The key to sustainability is finding "brand sponsorships" and crowdfunding is a marketing tool that will help pave the way:

> I think this is more to get people to discover the site and when we do go and find investors, we can show them—"over 700 people backed us with over $30,000. It must mean we're doing something right". We got so much press from it, and a lot of people found the site that didn't know it existed before. So besides getting money, Kickstarter is a great place to get yourself discovered.
>
> ($30,500 USD, Kickstarter)

By doing this, one could argue these journalists are in fact "commodifying" their donors. The theory of the audience commodity goes back to the sociologist Dallas Smythe (1981). He argued that the commodity produced by media was not the show, or the broadcast, but rather the audience, which was then sold to advertisers in the form of ratings. Further, and this is where his theory gets contested, Smythe argued that the audience was actually working by paying attention to advertisements. The television or radio programme was simply the "free lunch" offered as an enticement, to suck the audience in so they would do the real work of paying attention to advertisements that were instructing them in what to buy. This idea of a free lunch is a reference to a practice some bars will undertake where they offer free food as a way to get patrons through their doors to drink, which is where they really make their money. (There's a reason cheap wing night exists at the pub.) As Pridmore and Trottier (2014) describe, the type of work audiences engage in is an "immaterial form of labour," in other words they're not making anything, but through paying attention to advertisements audiences are working at learning "to buy goods and to spend their income accordingly" (p. 139). Key to Smythe's theory was that audiences may be labouring, without explicit knowledge that they are doing so (Pridmore & Trottier, 2014). In other words, even if you don't know you're working, you can still be working.

This theory of the audience commodity was—and continues to be—controversial, principally around this question of whether audiences actually work. Consuming media, even advertising, is often thought of as a leisure activity, something people do for fun. One only has to look at the hoopla that surrounds the advertisements on Superbowl Sunday in the United States to understand that advertisements can be seen as entertainment in themselves. It's not only football fans who tune in to watch the final game of the American National Football League, there are people who only turn on the television for the ads.

Some also argue that an audience commodity analysis downplays audience agency (Caraway, 2011). The idea here is that audiences aren't necessarily passive consumers. We are not stupid. We are critical thinkers who know when we are being sold a product and can make decisions for ourselves about where to best spend our money. We also understand when we watch a streaming service like Netflix that doesn't have explicit ads, that there is product placement in all these shows. We're able to tell when a character drives a certain car or wears certain clothes that it's an ad, that a company has paid to have those products show up on the programme.

In the case of crowdfunding, the question of whether donors are working and what type of agency they might have could be similarly contested. As mentioned, the role of the donor is often positioned as one that is empowering—audiences have the opportunity to put their money behind journalism they feel is worthwhile. They can have an impact on journalism, and by extension democracy. However, while this may be the case during the initial crowdfunding campaign, what this book asks the reader to consider is that when journalists are hoping to leverage donor interest into proof to advertisers there is an audience for their work, they are effectively looking to sell their audience to advertisers. The expectation is this audience will eventually work by paying attention to advertisements and learn to become consumers.

At the same time, however, the relationship journalists have with their funders is more complicated than simply leveraging them into advertiser dollars. Many of the journalists described crowdfunding as building a community around their project. On one hand, pragmatically, developing a community was about getting themselves and their work exposure. As one journalist who was raising money for an online magazine put it, "crowdfunding is not only about funding, but it's also building a community that will help us get our project known" ($11,700 USD, Kickstarter). But on the other hand, the idea of community is also described altruistically—they want donors to be engaged with their work and start meaningful dialogues about the stories they are covering. As will be explored in the next chapter, most journalists feel a strong sense of responsibility towards their funders.

As with crowdfunding, crowdsourcing is also often positioned as something positive, in that it engages the audience actively in the news process; audiences are contributing to democracy by lending their expertise, helping sift through data, or sharing their stories (Aitamurto, 2016; Bradshaw & Brightwell, 2012). But it is also work. Perhaps it is easier to make a direct connection between crowdsourcing and work if someone is helping a journalist to sort through data and find stories, but sharing personal stories and expert opinions with a journalist is also work. Even if talking to a journalist may not seem like work in the way it is typically imagined, there is time, energy, and thought that goes into participating in an interview, whether it's to share your personal experience or your expertise.

There is also another kind of labour that needs to be acknowledged when journalists use social media to reach out to sources, one that has far-reaching implications that go beyond journalism to encompass much of our online lives. Fuchs (2012) uses the term "prosumer commodities" to describe social media users who fill up these spaces with their creative work, whose data are then collected and sold to advertisers. Rather than positioning social media as a democratizing and empowering force, one that fosters creativity, Fuchs counters that social media is actually working towards the "total commodification of human creativity" (p. 56). Thinking about crowdsourcing through the lens of the prosumer commodity theory, journalists who use social media to crowdsource are in fact working for these social media companies. Similarly, people who use social media sites to respond to journalists, or send journalists pictures or video from events they are witnessing, are also working for these sites. Social media platforms would not exist without input from audiences, and anyone who uses these sites is being tracked and targeted for ads. While social media can be useful tools, it's important to remember that using these sites for the work of journalism is not benign, but in fact contributing to the profits of large corporations.

Aside from the question of whether crowdsourcing lines the pockets of social media companies, some also question how much agency crowdsourcing actually affords audiences in the first place. As Aitamurto (2016) rightly points out, in crowdsourcing "the locus of power lies within the process organizer—the crowdsourcer—who conducts the crowdsourcing initiative" (p. 328). Although audiences have the opportunity to shape journalism through their expertise or help, ultimately it is the journalist who initiates and directs the process. While audience input guides journalists and shapes stories, as evidenced through the Australian Broadcasting Corporation example earlier in this chapter, it is ultimately the journalist who makes the final decisions about what is news and what isn't.

## Conclusion

Crowdfunding through single-campaign platforms such as Kickstarter and Indiegogo is extremely labour-intensive. Both the design of the campaign and the outreach involved takes a great deal of time and energy, requiring journalists to tap into their networks of families, friends, and colleagues. While larger organizations that use crowdfunding as one part of their funding structure will hire people specifically to deal with this, the process of asking for money on a single-campaign public platform can make journalists who are not used to dealing with marketing and publicity uncomfortable. Having to become entrepreneurs who are effectively "selling" their idea to a wider public is at odds with the work routines and norms most journalists are used to. As Kawamoto (2003) describes: "In traditional news organizations, there is a metaphorical firewall between the advertising and editorial functions of a news medium" (p. 23). In crowdfunding this wall between the money and the journalists no longer exits; what journalists are able to create depends entirely on how well they market and sell their ideas. While some journalists have embraced being transparent and public about their process, seeing this as part of the move to involve audiences more in the news process, many feel very awkward about asking for money and marketing their work. Some research has found that younger journalists are more comfortable with the process than older journalists (Aitamurto, 2011), however, in this research both less experienced and more experienced journalists felt awkward about marketing their work, or as one journalist described who was raising money to support his freelancing, having to "ask for permission" from the public before beginning their reporting ($2,200 USD, Kickstarter). This move towards entrepreneurial journalism goes against the norms under which most journalists are used to operating.

Many of these journalists are engaging in what Kuehn and Corrigan (2013) call "hope" labour. As they describe, hope labour is "un- or under-compensated work carried out in the present, often for experience or exposure, in the hope that future employment opportunities may follow" (p. 21). Most of the journalists who were crowdfunding on single campaign platforms said they do not make a lot of money from crowdfunding and do not see it as a sustainable long-term way to raise funding. Rather, they were hoping that crowdfunding would be the start of full-time employment. If they were raising funds to start an online publication, many were hoping that they will be able to make this their full-time job by securing advertising or large investor funding. Essentially these journalists were hoping to "sell" their donors to advertisers, making the case that advertisers should invest in their publication, because they have a proven audience. This can all be seen through Dallas Smythe's lens of the "audience commodity," where donors will become audiences, who will then work paying attention to advertisements. As discussed, theories of the audience commodity are controversial. With crowdfunding the case could be made that donors are freely giving their attention and their money to journalists and this is empowering. But this agency becomes murkier as journalists hope to leverage donor attention into advertising revenue.

In the case of journalists who were starting their careers, and more seasoned freelancers, they were hoping that crowdfunding would bolster sagging freelance budgets and allow them to either get their start as a journalist, or continue as freelancers. While in one sense this could be characterized as empowering, in another, drawing on Cohen's (2012, 2016) research into the exploitation of freelance journalists, crowdfunding is also a way for news organizations to get more work out of freelance employees for less money. If freelancers are turning to crowdfunding, and all the labour this entails, in order to make freelancing financially viable, news organizations that use this form of journalism are profiting from unpaid labour.

Similarly, crowdsourcing can also be very labour-intensive, requiring planning to organize the best approach and the best form of outreach. There is also work involved in maintaining connections with people and responding to those who reach out. Crowdsourcing also requires journalists to be open about their work in a way they may not be used to. Many journalists are used to keeping a story under wraps until it is time to go public. This is especially true with investigative journalism. However, this journalism norm is changing as some journalists are finding there are advantages to being open about their work, and even who they are; it can help with finding new sources, promoting their work and laying claim to a story. Finally, any discussion of crowd-sourcing would be remiss if it did not acknowledge the work of the audience. The argument can be made that both audiences and jour-nalists are "prosumer commodities" (Fuchs, 2012), working at filling up social media sites with content. In addition, while crowdsourcing is often positioned as empowering for audiences, giving them a voice in the news process, it should not be forgotten that audiences are working when they help create journalism. Even sharing a personal story or experience, no matter how empowering it feels, is still work that requires time and energy. Any accounting of the labour of journalism can't forget these important contributions, no matter how willingly they are offered.

# 3 Identity

## Introduction

When you read a story on the *Guardian*'s website, a pop-up window appears at the end asking you to donate. Their pitch to you is that reader support enables their reporting to be autonomous and independent:

> Our editorial independence and autonomy allows us to provide fearless investigations and analysis of those with political and commercial power. We can give a voice to the oppressed and neglected, and help bring about a brighter, fairer future. Your support protects this.
>
> (Pengelly, 2020)

There are similar promises on the web pages of other news organizations that rely on support from crowdfunding. At *The Tyee* reader support means they can "stay completely focused on publishing truly valuable journalism for our readers, instead of being driven to sell advertising" (*Tyee*, n.d., para 4). Similarly, journalists crowdfunding on one-off crowdfunding platforms such as Kickstarter and Indiegogo often position their pitch as a promise for independent journalism. The unifying thread: donor support means they won't have to rely as much, or at all, on advertising or corporate support. However, if the audience is now a financial investor in the news, what changes in the relationship between audience and journalist? How does the professional identity of the journalist shift when they solicit funding directly from their potential audience?

This chapter focuses on the different ways that journalists who crowdfund identify professionally in relation to the journalistic norms of autonomy and independence (Coddington, 2015; Deuze, 2011), how they characterize their relationships with funders, and ethical concerns that arise. This chapter looks at whether crowdfunding journalists can maintain autonomy and independence while simultaneously trying to attract donors. It will address the different ways journalists negotiate their relationships with donors, from those who construct invisible "walls" (Coddington, 2015) between the money and the story, stating outright that they will not be swayed by the audience, to those who feel this is not even an issue that needs considering, because donors know exactly who they are putting their money behind and agree with their point of view. This chapter also explores the different ways crowdfunding journalists identify in relation to the journalistic norm of "fairness and balance" (Deuze, 2011; Gasher, Skinner, & Coulter, 2020). While some were striving to maintain this norm, others are crowdfunding as a way to create advocacy journalism that had a distinct agenda. Then there are the journalists I call journalists with a "point of view," who feel they can report accurately and truthfully, yet still take a distinct position on issues.

In terms of crowdsourcing, this chapter examines how journalists view and negotiate their relationships with the "crowd." Crowdsourcing is often characterized as empowering for audiences in that they get to participate in the news process (Aitamurto, 2016), but drawing on the crowd for help in telling stories, whether as witnesses, experts, or to sort through data, also raises questions about this relationship. Journalists, of course, are used to interviewing people as sources for a story, but when you're explicitly asking for help to cover a story, what does this change? This chapter also examines how crowdsourcing intersects with the journalistic norm of verification and considers circumstances where transparency is becoming more valued (Singer, 2015).

## Crowdfunding: imagined walls

Journalism is a profession that is different from occupations such as medicine or law, in that there is no set exam that must be passed, or strict professional guidelines that must be followed, nor is there a requirement for formal education. Since the end of the Second World War there has been a proliferation of journalism schools and increasingly the expectation that journalists will have some kind of formal training, but the reality is that journalists can come from all walks of education. Nonetheless, a set of norms have developed around the profession (Deuze, 2011), or boundaries (Carlson & Lewis, 2015), that journalists use to define the work they do (Singer, 2015). One of the key norms in Western journalism is a commitment to autonomy and independence (Deuze, 2011; Singer, 2015). Deuze (2011) identifies autonomy as being widely accepted as one of the "ideal–typical values" that are part of "journalism's ideology," lending "legitimacy and credibility to what (journalists) do" (p. 20). Journalists expect "editorial autonomy, freedom and independence" (p. 21). Deuze does argue that in a multi-platform and multi-cultural environment, ideas of autonomy need to be rethought in some ways. Journalists working in these environments have to work with others and share information and resources. As well, "[th]e literature addressing multi-culturalism calls for more community-based reporting, signals the need for journalists to become much more aware of entrenched inequalities in society and expects media professionals to become active agents in reversing these" (p. 27). Deuze suggests, "autonomy in this context is collaborative (with colleagues and publics)" (p. 27). However, the idea of autonomy and independence from the influence of advertisers and media owners remains a prevalent norm. There has been much critical research that asserts that advertisers and owners of news organizations can exert pressure and influence newsrooms, both overtly and indirectly (Donsbach, 2012; Herman & Chomsky, 1988; McChesney, 2004). But traditionally most journalists are not directly involved in the financial matters of the organizations they work for, focusing instead on producing journalistic content. For journalists who have had careers in legacy media, ideas of autonomy are contingent on an imagined "wall" constructed between the content and commercial concerns. There are no physical walls of course, although some news organizations do make sure the two departments are kept separate, rather the wall is an idea, a metaphor constructed to remind journalists that they should operate without influence, in order to perform their jobs in impartial, fair, and balanced ways. The idea is that journalists should only be loyal to the pursuit of the story they are chasing and are not to be swayed by outside financial forces. In this sense, these imagined walls remind journalists that there is a sense of nobility attached to the profession; it is a public service, an important part of a functioning democracy. With crowdfunding, however, journalists have no choice but to be directly involved in the financial aspects of their own work, which sets up a troublesome dilemma—how can journalists remain independent in their reporting, at the same time that they are trying to attract funders? What happens to this imagined wall as well as notions of impartiality and autonomy when a crowdfunding journalist has to attract and keep funders happy?

## Autonomy

Business researchers talk about the need for crowdfunders to build a community and "form ties with the crowd" in order for a campaign to be successful (Belleflame, Lambert, & Schwienbacher, 2014, p. 588). The implication is that the crowd must be invested in order to invest. The language of relationship and community building is often part of the fabric of pitches news organizations and individual journalists make. For instance, on its "about" page, *The Tyee* describes its readers as valued, and assures them their thoughts are taken seriously and have meaningful impact:

> You are a communicative bunch, for which we're grateful. You tell us what you think—and what you want from us—through story comments, surveys, phone calls, the articles you choose to read and share. Many of our articles arise from your suggestions or are improved by your input.
>
> *(Tyee, n.d., para 2)*

The pitch goes on to directly identify that there is a relationship, one that can be deepened by giving contact information or money. But this is not a one-way friendship, in return donors will continue to be listened to and see their shared values reflected in the journalism:

> You are invited to deepen the relationship by subscribing to one or more of our email newsletters, and by supporting us financially by becoming a Tyee Builder. In return, we pledge to keep listening in order to produce journalism reflecting the values we share—a deep concern for truth-telling, justice, the environment and holding power accountable. We exist to serve you (not advertisers, hedge fund owners or political agendas).
>
> *(Tyee, n.d., para 3)*

The message about the relationship that is conveyed through this type of language is one of mutual respect. But it also brings up questions about what influence funders have, if the organization exists to serve them. *The Tyee* deals with this by being very explicit on its website that it is committed to independence and focused on fact-based journalism. Similarly, the *Texas Tribune*, which also uses crowdfunding as one part of its financial plan, sets clear expectations about how its reporters undertake their reporting, stating unequivocally that they are dedicated to impartial journalism:

> Our fundraisers inform all potential donors—individuals, foundations, corporate sponsors, underwriters—that their contributions to the Tribune do not entitle them to preferential treatment or to

relationships with newsroom staff, and in no way protect them from investigations or scrutiny.

(*Texas Tribune*, n.d., para 11)

Similarly, journalists who are crowdfunding on single campaign platforms also try to set boundaries between funders and the journalism they produce. They try to maintain a sense of distance from their funders in terms of editorial control. One journalist, who crowdfunded for an online magazine that focuses on architecture and the urban environment, said they do take money from funders who would be interested in the work they do, but they stress that funders will have no influence over the direction of their reporting:

> When it comes to us—who has money who cares about what we do? Often times its developers, real estate developers and so they fund us. Not many of them, but a few do because they like what we do. Do we feel required or morally obligated to give them something back? Hard to say. We've tried to create a real understanding that that would not happen.
>
> ($20,000 USD, Kickstarter)

All of the journalists I spoke to held a similar view and said funders did not, or would not, ultimately have control over the content of the journalism they produced. They also said that it was the norm for funders to donate without putting any stipulations on the journalist. If they had, journalists said they would not feel obligated to comply or change their reporting in any way. Essentially, they constructed their own imagined walls between their content and their donors. However, unlike the larger news organizations cited above, none of them formulated clearly articulated policies that they communicated to their funders. Rather, they created rules for themselves as they went along, inventing measures to ensure there was no real or perceived conflict of interest. One journalist, who raised money to support reporting in an independent online publication, said he once returned a $20 (USD) donation from a city supervisor on a story to do with the city budget. The supervisor was potentially a source and although it was a small amount, the journalist felt it had to be returned. "It was only twenty dollars, but we thought that would create a sense of impropriety" ($19,400 USD, Spot.us). Another freelance journalist who crowdfunded to support a series that ran in an independent online publication tried to distance himself from the funders by not checking the donor list throughout the process:

I know a lot of people in the community. I wanted to have a little bit of a sense of distance with the process, especially asking people directly for money. This project was writing about people I did not know, so I didn't necessarily feel that I would be unduly influenced by anybody who funded it. But I did have a slight sense of unease about putting a face to a dollar amount and feeling that I had to take the project in a certain direction.

($2,200 USD, Kickstarter)

This journalist said the method he came up with made him feel more comfortable about the process and helped him feel confident that he was not being unduly influenced.

There was one journalist who made the argument that crowdfunding might present less of a problem than funding journalism through foundation support, a source of income many non-profits depend on. This journalist made the point that with crowdfunding "interests are spread out over a lot of different people" rather than relying on funding from "one foundation or one grant that has really specific guidelines" (journalist, $6,900 USD, Kickstarter). For this journalist, who was crowdfunding to create an online magazine, distributed funding meant there was less potential that journalists would be pressured to mould their reporting in a certain direction.

Journalists who had worked in the commercial news industry did compare the distance they tried to maintain from funders with how things usually operate in legacy media. In their experience, journalists work largely without any direct concern for how the media organization is funded, and there is a firm dividing line between editorial content and advertising. While they acknowledge that the wants and needs of advertisers can influence the content or overall direction of a publication, they never felt like they directly experienced such pressure in their professional lives, nor would they ever want to. They brought this same expectation into the process of crowdfunding.

However, despite wanting to create a sense of distance and autonomy from funders in terms of editorial control, journalists also feel a strong sense of responsibility towards their funders to create the work that was promised and to do it well. As one journalist who was crowdfunding to create an online publication said:

I care deeply about doing a good job for them because in a very real way, they cumulatively change the way I live my life. It was this, like a deep appreciation that I probably don't feel for many other people besides my wife.

(\$95,500 USD, Kickstarter)

Those with experience of working for legacy media described this responsibility as being more intense than the sense of responsibility they have felt in those environments. As one journalist said, "I didn't want people to feel as if they've wasted their money. And that is a very new thing – the idea that you want people to feel pleased by what they've contributed to" (journalist, \$15,000 CAD, Indiegogo). Another journalist described feeling immense pressure and said it was a steep "learning curve" to get used to not only being accountable to editors, but also the 200 people who had funded her (\$6,900 USD, Kickstarter).

The imagined walls these journalists constructed have the potential to be further complicated by the fact they were also eager to engage with their funders. First, pragmatically, they were interested in creating a dialogue with their funders in order to build an audience. But beyond building a loyal following, they were also genuinely interested in what their audience thought about the stories they were investigating, including being open to taking suggestions for story ideas and story treatments. That said, only one of the journalists I spoke to, who was raising money to support his freelancing, had actively sought consultations with his donors, offering a consultation as part of the rewards system:

> It [the consultation] was actually very helpful to me because it gave me ideas that I hadn't thought of. I don't have to do what he [the funder] says because he's not my boss. I promised only a consultation … If he wanted me to do something I couldn't do, I just wouldn't do it. But his feedback was actually useful.
>
> (\$33,000 USD, Kickstarter)

This journalist said the donor had interesting ideas and questions that he had not thought of. Given this positive experience, offering consultations is something he would likely do more often.

It's complicated to have this sense of responsibility towards donors, but still want to keep them at arm's length. One journalist who was raising money to start an online publication observed that while ultimately this was a business transaction, there was a strong feeling of thankfulness:

> It's weird because on one hand they're investing in your company. But on the other hand, they're investing through a platform where

that's the main purpose of the platform. So you don't really owe them anything except for what you've promised them. We want to make them [donors] feel like they're appreciated. But at the same time, once the reward has been fulfilled … that's all the relationship is between you and them. But we're always going to have a reverence for them, if that makes sense.

($30,500 USD, Kickstarter)

Overall, the journalists in this research held onto autonomy as an "ideal–typical" value (Deuze, 2011). They wanted to maintain editorial control over their work and keep the influence of their funders at bay. But at the same time, this ideal was complicated by the fact they felt a great deal of responsibility towards their funders. Trying to create editorial distance, at the same time as needing to draw in donors as part of a community, created tension for many entrepreneurial journalists. On the one hand, they felt very grateful and beholden to their funders, but on the other, this was still a professional relationship of sorts. While these are seemingly contradictory impulses—autonomy and responsibility—the journalists I spoke to were confident that the direction their reporting takes would not be influenced by what funders wanted, rather the responsibility they felt was to produce quality journalism, in terms of delivering what they promised in their pitches.

## Objectivity, fairness, and balance

A journalist's sense of identity is often tied to being a public servant, someone who is committed to factual, independent reporting that they see as imperative in a functioning democracy (Hunter, O'Donnell, & Cohen, forthcoming). One way that journalists have approached autonomy is to try to take an "objective" or "fair and balanced" approach to their reporting (Gasher, Skinner, & Coulter, 2020; Winston & Winston, 2021). While some journalists and researchers who study the practice of journalism question the effectiveness and importance of these ideas, others argue that objectivity "remains a foundational premise" (St. John III & Johnson, 2012, p. 3) that underlies much of how mainstream news is structured and organized. It is a norm that is largely accepted as "commonsense" (Kaplan, 2012, p. 26). While objectivity is often identified as a distinctly American way of thinking about journalism that does not necessarily translate into other parts of the world (Schudson & Anderson, 2009), others argue that it is an ideal that has spread beyond North America and is widely seen as foundational (Jirik, 2012; St. John III & Johnson, 2012).

The origins of objectivity are disputed. Its roots have been traced back to the commercial penny press of the nineteenth century that aimed to be politically neutral in an effort to appeal to everyone and capture the largest audience (St. John III & Johnson, 2012; Stephens, 2007). Others point to technological changes, specifically the rise of the telegraph, as giving rise to a need for an economical style of writing that emphasized essential facts, rather than descriptive writing (Emery & Emery, 1996). Others make the point that objectivity was solidified as a journalistic norm as journalism became increasingly professionalized in the early twenty-first century in America (Schudson, 2001), and although it is a complicated and contested term, it has served to create a sense of solidarity and professional distinction (Schudson & Anderson, 2009). As Schudson (2001) describes, the norm of objectivity "guides journalists to separate facts from values and to report only the facts" (p. 150). The job of the journalist is to report "something called 'news' without commenting on it, slanting it, or shaping its formulation in any way" (p. 150). Similarly, Calcutt and Hammond (2011) divide objectivity into three distinct but closely related ideas: (1) truthfulness, a commitment to reporting information that is factually correct; (2) neutrality, striving for fairness, balance, and impartiality; and (3) detachment, separating "fact from comment" (p. 98). Essentially, objective journalists are expected to be dispassionate, and to put aside their own emotions and allegiances when reporting.

Objectivity has been harshly critiqued, notably relatively early on by Tuchman (1972), as a "strategic ritual" that limits the range of viewpoints offered to the public, and as an unattainable and undesirable goal in a world where there are many variations of the "truth" (Maras, 2013; Winston & Winston, 2021). Moreover, objectivity has been dismissed as simply impossible because of "human fallibility" (Calcutt & Hammond, 2011, p. 98). Journalists cannot help but be affected by their social background and history, regardless of best efforts to remain impartial (Winston & Winston, 2021). Others have pointed out that the way objectivity is taught and expected to be practised is particularly impossible for journalists of colour. In Radiyah Chowdhury's award-winning essay "The forever battle of a journalist of colour,"[1] the Canadian journalist wrote about how she first learned about ideas of objectivity in journalism school: "Objectivity as it was presented to us seemed to be tailored for a specific type of person, one whose capacity to be dispassionate about certain issues came from a place of privilege that was unfamiliar to me" (2020, para 2). Further, in the essay she writes that:

[t]hese days, it feels like Canadian journalism asks something almost impossible of people of colour. It asks them to set aside the traumas they face on a daily basis for the sake of an industry largely created by white people.

(para 3)

The essay goes on to describe the impossibility of separating herself from the story:

To be racialized is to be politicized. I could walk into any room as a journalist, but by virtue of my headscarf I'd be recognized as a Muslim woman first. I was taught to present both sides of a story, but what would I do in situations where one of those sides threatened my ability to live peacefully in a democratic society, like the secularism law passed in Quebec?[2] ... It seemed like at some point, the sacrifice I'd make to be a mainstream journalist would be to quiet the human side of myself. In fact, I would have to work twice as hard to be considered a fair journalist, lest I be accused of bias by way of my ethnicity and faith.

(Chowdhury, 2020, para 4)

Others say the notion of objectivity is misunderstood by its critics, and that it should not be thought of as synonymous with balance. As Tom Rosenteil, the Director of the American Press Institute, argues, the intent of objectivity was not to suggest that journalists did not have bias:

Actually it was just the opposite The idea migrated from the sciences to journalism as a sophisticated response to the discovery of unconscious bias in reporting ... The idea was that journalists needed to employ objective, observable, repeatable methods of verification in their reporting—precisely because they could never be personally objective. Their methods of reporting had to be objective because they never could be.

(Rosenteil, 2020b, 2020c)

Rosenteil argues further that objective inquiry—objective reporting—was not supposed to be equated with "mindlessly giving both sides equal treatment, thinking there are just two sides to a story" (Rosenteil, 2020d). Rather, considering multiple points of view, being transparent in reporting methods, making sure to verify your reporting, is what objectivity was trying to get at. As he writes: "Far from denying personal background, this kind of inquiry recognizes that people's background always enriches their journalism" (Rosenteil, 2020e). His concern with a quick dismissal of the idea of objectivity is that "[i]f journalists replace a flawed understanding of objectivity by taking refuge in subjectivity and think their opinions have more moral integrity than genuine inquiry, journalism will be lost" (Rosenteil, 2020f).

The crowdfunding journalists I spoke to took a variety of approaches to these ideas of objectivity, fairness, and balance. While some journalists, all of whom had attended journalism school and worked in legacy media, still adhered to these norms, most positioned themselves as at odds with these ideas. They either rejected these norms outright, calling themselves advocacy journalists, or described their journalism as a hybrid that does not see factual reporting as something that is in conflict with a distinct "point of view."

## Advocacy journalism, point of view, and impartiality

Some journalists described themselves outright as advocacy journalists, meaning their journalism came from a situated perspective and they were not concerned with impartiality, or covering a story from multiple points of view. Other journalists, while not positioning themselves as advocacy journalists, described their journalism as having a "point of view." This point of view can manifest in an interest in certain types of stories (environmental, human rights, etc.) or a political perspective (progressive, conservative, etc.). However, while these journalists did not try to suppress their point of view, they also said they strive to report accurately. They do not see these two notions—accuracy and point of view—as contradictory or mutually exclusive. For instance, one freelance journalist, who described himself as having a point of view, said he is not an advocacy journalist, because he feels these types of journalists will prioritize their agenda over facts. "I'm not going to suppress something that's true, just because it serves my outlook on things. I would not do that, because to me that's dishonest. I think one can be opinionated and honest at the same time" ($33,200 USD, Kickstarter). As an example, this journalist said when covering wars some conflicts can be murky, but when it comes to American soldiers fighting the Taliban he said, "there's no way that I'm going to be equally sympathetic to both sides. I wouldn't try to be and I wouldn't pretend to be." Another journalist said in his independent publication they allow their writers to "present points of view and personality," yet they still strive to get at some form of "truth" through analytic journalism, by looking at "what's really at play" in a story ($20,000 USD, Indiegogo). He was adamant they are not advocacy journalists, pointing out that his organization is part of the Investigative News Network that would not have let them join if they were purely advocacy journalists. He went on to say that if his publication wanted to advocate for something they would do it the way "journalists have always done it," by exposing and telling stories that have not been told.

There were some journalists who talked about adhering strongly to notions of impartiality and said they strove to put aside their personal points of view when reporting. One journalist, who freelances for legacy media, said the way she sees it, advocacy journalists try to change situations by reporting on them. She believes the job of a journalist is to shed "light" on an issue, rather than try to affect change and that any attempts to manipulate a situation through reporting "falls outside the purview of a journalist" ($15,000 CAD, Kickstarter). Her job is not to change a situation but rather to "illuminate the problem." Another American journalist, who crowdfunded to support his own website, said he had always been personally opposed to the war in Afghanistan, but when it came to reporting, he tried to be fair and set aside his biases:

> Overall, I'm still against it (the war) but to be fair I had to come back and talk about how there are roads now. There are cell phone towers. There's construction. Yes, that all comes with a lot of corruption and a lot of it's not done well, but these are decided improvements and it's important to mention them and talk about them. I feel that if I were a really biased unfair reporter then I would just omit those things or I would lie about them.
>
> ($26,000 USD, Kickstarter)

This journalist described it as important to his integrity as a professional journalist to consider many angles to a story. These journalists who talked about impartiality in relation to their work adhered strongly to notions of truthfulness, by which they meant factual reporting, neutrality, and detachment (Calcutt & Hammond, 2011), seeing these elements as essential to their identity as journalists. Interestingly, all these journalists had worked for legacy media organizations that required them to adhere to these notions of fairness and balance in their reporting, and they had brought these ideals over into their crowdfunding ventures. Striving for impartiality and factual reporting was important to them, and were ideals they believed in strongly.

However, it is interesting that the majority of journalists I spoke to who were crowdfunding on single campaign platforms did not believe that objectivity was "a foundational premise" (St. John III & Johnson,

2012) of the news, or a norm that is simply "commonsense" (Kaplan, 2012). Those who identified themselves clearly as advocacy journalists with political views that guided their storytelling or strong attachments to the stories they were covering, said that objectivity is impossible and unwanted; in covering stories, they had an agenda they wanted to advance. They did not feel as if they would be doing a disservice to their funders by reporting this way, rather their funders knew exactly what they were supporting and held similar political or social views. The journalists who identified as advocacy journalists either had no previous journalism experience, or some experience with independent publications. They were not planning on having their reporting appear in legacy media, or any organization that might want journalists to adhere to impartiality. The journalists who identified as having a "point of view" were also aiming their journalism at independent publications. However, rather than identifying as advocates, they had internalized the journalistic norm of factual reporting—or "truthfulness" as Calcutt and Hammond (2011) describe. Marrying point of view with facts was not seen as a problematic. These journalists felt that you can be upfront about your point of view and create valuable journalism that presents facts as you see them. This includes being open to reporting facts that may conflict with, or serve to undermine, your own point of view. This approach aligns with the point that Rosenteil (2020a, 2020b, 2020c, 2020d, 2020e, 2020f) is trying to make, that objectivity has been misunderstood as being without bias, when really it should be thought of as an approach that carefully considers many points of view, but does not necessarily present them all as equal if it's not warranted.

## Crowdsourcing: independence

Crowdsourcing also raises questions about where journalists stand in relation to their audiences. As discussed in Chapter 2, some journalists who use Facebook and Twitter to reach out to potential sources feel a sense of obligation to respond to everyone who reaches out to them. They do so pragmatically, because they want to keep up these relationships so they can call on people at other times if needed, but more than this, they also feel grateful to the people who respond and want to acknowledge their efforts. One mid-career journalist said he cultivates a sense of community through social media, and considers many of his followers to be friends who have helped him with stories. However, all the journalists in this research were very clear that while they have respect for their sources and feel a duty to tell their stories responsibly, sources do not have a say over the direction a story takes.

At ProPublica, an organization that often uses crowdsourcing or what they call "engagement reporting" in their practices, they are very careful to state that they are independent from those who help them with their stories. They describe their audience engagement as an opportunity for audiences to share their stories and share their expertise:

> When you're directly affected by an issue, you often know a lot about it. You can have information, leads and stories. Sometimes, you've been trying to tell people and you've been ignored or over-looked in the process. Engagement reporting at ProPublica is about giving you a place to share that kind of information.
>
> (Tobin et al., 2019, para 1)

But while they may be offering audiences this opportunity, ProPublica is very clear that they are not advocacy journalists; they are independent journalists who are committed to looking at many sides of an issue. "At ProPublica, we aim for stories to have an impact. But we're journalists, not activists. That means we're independent—not aligned with any particular cause or position" (Tobin et al., 2019, para 5).

However, when asking for help from audiences, it can be difficult to keep those audiences at arm's length. As can happen with crowdfunding, a sense of responsibility can develop. For instance, the Australian Broadcasting Corporation reporters who were investigating long-term care homes described the people who helped them crowdsource stories as "legitimate collaborators." As they put it: "We want to make sure our reporting repays the trust our audience has put in us … That means listening to their stories, finding patterns, generating fresh data and, most importantly, finding ways to give back to them wherever possible" (Puccini, Prior, & Filali, 2018, paras 63, 65). That said, some journalists didn't see a difference between the responsibility they feel towards sources they find through crowdsourcing or other means. As one journalist described: "I would say it's the same sense of responsibility as any other source that you would talk to."

## Verification and transparency

When an earthquake hit Haiti in January 2010, CNN published tweets from people who were there describing what was unfolding, and from friends and family who were relating what their loved ones on the scene had told them. The accounts were harrowing: collapsed buildings, people trapped in the rubble, a picture of devastation and despair.

CNN wanted to publish, as quickly as possible, information that was coming in from the site of the disaster, but at the same time needed to make sure their readers understood that this information hadn't been independently verified by the news organization. To manage this, at the top of the story they ran this disclaimer: "CNN is monitoring tweets and other messages from people in Haiti and reports from those who said they have been in touch with friends and family. CNN has not been able to able to verify this material" (Simon, 2010).

Accuracy and verification is a hallmark of journalism (Hermida, 2017; Schudson & Anderson, 2009), but with crowdsourcing verification can become complicated. As reporter Mercedes Bunz wrote in 2010, "Up until now, journalism has been devoted to verified facts—but the crowd-sourced approach is generally not about using previously trusted sources" (para 10). For some events, particularly breaking news involving disasters, Bunz writes that the material coming in on social media can be "faster, more detailed and richer than the material provided by news agencies" (para 9). In the decade since, news organizations have adapted new policies when dealing with this type of material, often doing what CNN did in this situation, opting for transparency instead of verification, and running disclaimers that explain where information is coming from and clearly stating that it has not yet been verified.

Aitamurto (2016) describes a sense of "blended responsibility" that can emerge in cases where journalists can't verify everything and ask their readers to take this lack of verification into account. As an example, a newspaper in Sweden, *Svenska Dagbladet*, wanted to look into how mortgage rates differed across the country, asking readers to submit data from their area. Forty thousand people responded. At first, journalists tried to verify everything they were receiving, but after reaching out to about 80 people, the process became overwhelming. There was simply too much, so instead the newspaper let readers know not everything was fact-checked and they would need to take this into account. As Aitamurto writes: "The situation reflects not only a balance of traditional journalistic norms with new open procedures, but a balance of responsibility between readers and journalists—a kind of blended responsibility" (2016, p. 291).

However, when journalists crowdsource through Twitter or Facebook to find sources to interview, vetting is still part of the process. One mid-career freelance journalist said that for people working in daily news, vetting people they connect with through crowdsourcing is very important. As she described:

> I think in this saturated media environment online people care less about beating the other outlet. I think almost the bigger challenge

now is "do we have it right". I know that's a journalism cliché, but I think when you're dealing with an environment of so much misinformation ... that is a higher priority now. So you even just want to be careful of who you find when you crowdsource and be able to vet them.

Another mid-career freelance journalist said she may Google someone, or see if they have any social connections in common. She might also check to see how many followers they have. However, she cautions that having a lot of followers does not automatically mean a person should be seen as more legitimate:

I don't want to say that and have it be interpreted as "if they have a ton of followers, therefore their opinion matters more, their experience is more real," because I think that would further inhibit us from actually reaching real people who are really experiencing issues we are talking about and living their lives. But you can get a sense (of a person), even from looking at their Twitter feed or what comes up from them on Google. You learn about people. Depending on what they Tweet and how transparent they are about their lives, you do sort of have an open notebook situation with people if you can see them on social media.

However, she also cautioned that what you see on social media may not be an accurate reflection of a person's experience; people create social media personas, curating their social media to present themselves in certain ways, and journalists need to be cognizant that a person's online presentation may be very different from how they are offline.

### *Ambient awareness*

The content on Twitter or Facebook is sometimes dismissed as inconsequential or unreliable, a way to get bits of information out quickly, but hardly something through which we can understand complex ideas or events. Others counter that over time one can build accurate, complex narratives through a site like Twitter, through "ambient awareness" (Thompson, 2008). Think of a pixelated picture. Up close it looks like nothing but thousands of dots, but stand back and adjust your eyes, and the individual dots work together to create a unified picture. Similarly, on Twitter when you follow someone, even if they only post seemingly mundane bits of information about their lives, such as what they ate for lunch or the cute thing their pet did, over time you can build a complex picture of who they are and gain a sense of the rhythm of their life (Thompson, 2008). In the context of journalism, Hermida (2010) refers to this as "ambient journalism," the idea that the value of a tweet "does not lie in each individual fragment of news and information, but rather in the mental portrait created by a number of messages over time" (p. 301). In a sense, verification through a social media site like Twitter can also work like this. One tweet alone from a news event, such as an earthquake or a protest, perhaps doesn't tell you much, and its accuracy could be questioned. But if you put together tens, hundreds, or even thousands of tweets describing an event, a bigger picture can emerge that is unified, but still nuanced and complex.

## Conclusions

The journalistic norm of autonomy is one that crowdfunding journalists in this research felt very strongly about, but it is difficult to navigate as they also feel an incredible amount of responsibility towards their funders and want to create work their funders will find worthwhile. Some are also very interested in building a community with their funders and engaging with them. At the same time, they strive to keep funders at arm's length from any sort of editorial control, preferring they remain as "passive investors" (Schwienbacher & Larralde, 2012). It is a fine balance to maintain autonomy from funders while still maintaining a relationship with them. Further to this, while journalists may want editorial control, there is a power imbalance in this relationship as funders are essential to whether a project has the means to go ahead. While journalists said they strive very hard to maintain autonomy, there is the possibility journalists are being influenced by funders regardless of their best intentions, shaping crowdfunding campaigns to attract as large a pool of funders as possible. Journalists certainly put a lot of thought into how to attract an audience, creating catchy videos, offering rewards they hope will entice donations, and also looking for stories they hope will resonate with an audience. One concern about crowdfunding is that relying on what the "crowd" deems important or interesting means journalism could become a popularity contest, with worthwhile stories going unfunded and unreported. As one journalist who was crowdfunding to create his own website said, he was sure the reason his campaign was successful was because Kickstarter found it interesting and decided to put it on the front page, which significantly boosted his visibility ($26,000 USD, Kickstarter).

Journalism, by its very nature, is concerned with the audience; journalists are creating something to be read and consumed, and as such produce their work with an audience in mind. Many journalists think of themselves as providing a public service—they consider themselves watchdogs, holding governments and corporations to account. However, it is a subtle, but important shift from thinking *about* your audience, to thinking *about pleasing* your audience. Crowdfunding brings up difficult ethical questions in this regard. Some of the larger journalism organizations who crowdfund are very explicitly writing out their policies about editorial independence, however journalists taking on smaller, one-off campaigns often are not. Although journalists identify with the norm of autonomy, exactly how autonomy is to be achieved and maintained with crowdfunding is murky. As one journalist said, crowdfunding on these platforms is new for journalists and there is no consensus on how one should proceed. When journalists are entrepreneurs at the same time that they are reporters, "we as journalists and journalism educators are going to have to look at new rules for this" (journalist, $10,500 USD, Kickstarter). As Singer (2015) writes about entrepreneurial journalism more broadly, the boundaries that journalists used to call upon when defending or defining their profession are now called into question: "the point that successful innovation hinges on overlap among the needs of customers, content producers, and financiers explicitly calls into question the nature and viability of boundaries separating them" (p. 30). Coddington (2015) even questions how relevant this idea of the "wall" is today, going so far as to say that although "the wall maintains an iconic place in the American journalistic imagination … its era as a dominant norm is over" (pp. 78–79). Perhaps it's not realistic, at a time when journalism industries are struggling and journalists are looking for ways to survive, to insist on this strict boundary that cannot be crossed. As Coddington writes: "The erosion of this boundary is not necessarily something to be mourned. For decades, it has provided a means for journalists to avoid knowledge of and moral responsibility of the creeping co-option of their work by commercial interests" (p. 79).

As other political economic scholars of the media have continued to document and theorize over the years, despite the metaphor of the wall, advertisers and owners of news organizations can and do exert pressure on what appears in the news and how newsrooms operate, both overtly and less directly (Herman & Chomsky, 1988; Hunter, 2015; McChesney, 2004). In other words, despite the best efforts of individual journalists, the wall is not as steady or impervious as we like to imagine. Even so, as Coddington (2015) writes, "the wall has also carried significant practical consequences in giving journalists a symbolic image to remind them of their own role in maintaining a professional practice that fundamentally serves democratic aims rather than commercial ones" (p. 79).

While journalists in this research clearly identified with the norm of autonomy, the objectivity norm was less enthusiastically embraced. While some journalists hold on to ideals of impartiality, fairness, and balance in their reporting, the majority spoke of objectivity and impartiality as undesirable. Rather, they very clearly identify reporting as a human process that will never be neutral, as it involves people who cannot ever be fully divorced from their values, perspectives, and cultural milieus, nor should they. Many saw no contradiction between point of view and accurate reporting. Factual reporting with a "point of view" may be a notion that will be hard to accept for journalists schooled in the traditions of fairness, balance, and emotional and political detachment from stories. However, with the increase of user-generated content and the proliferation of sources of information online, notions of journalistic objectivity are arguably in the midst of another shift, as we see the rise of more news outlets that gear their products towards particular audiences. St. John III and Johnson (2012) point to websites like the Huffington Post and Salon.com that "take the news and craft it to appeal to the political, social, and economic interests of niche audiences" (p. 5). These crowdfunding journalists who say they can marry "point of view" with factual reporting are perhaps indicative of, and part of, an evolving journalistic norm, one in which these two notions are not mutually exclusive. In the United States, Canada, and other parts of the world, the Black Lives Matter movement has drawn attention to the notion that journalists should not separate themselves from the story and try to look for balance, because all points of view should not be treated equally. The job of the journalist is not to divorce themselves from the story, but weigh the facts and points of view that they find, and acknowledge when some have more weight than others (Lowery, 2020). As William Lowery wrote in the *New York Times*:

> For years, I've been among a chorus of mainstream journalists who have called for our industry to abandon the appearance of objectivity as the aspirational journalistic standard, and for reporters instead to focus on being fair and telling the truth, as best as one can, based on the given context and available facts.
>
> (2020, para 12)

When crowdsourcing, journalists adhere strongly to the notion of autonomy and remaining independent in their reporting, but there are times when they feel like they are negotiating new types of relationships with sources. As audiences share stories they can become, in a sense, collaborators, and journalists feel an obligation to listen carefully, honour, and respect their contributions. This is similar to how some crowdfunding journalists describe wanting to please their funders. There is a sense of gratitude that develops and from this comes a strong sense of responsibility, however this doesn't translate into audience influence over a story's direction.

The reputation of a journalist and the trust people place in them, is traditionally very much tied to the accuracy of their reporting, but with crowdsourcing, the journalistic norm of verification can become more complex. Thanks to social media, most notably Twitter, journalists can report quickly, in "real time," as events unfold, instead of having to wait until their allotted slot in the nightly newscast. While this means news breaks much more quickly, as Hermida (2017) writes, this can also be problematic. In an accelerated news cycle mistakes happen: "News organizations and journalists have shared erroneous rumours, misidentified suspects, and declared politicians and celebrities dead on social media" (p. 409). To mitigate this, some news organizations and journalists are cautious when reporting crowdsourced material. Transparency is key in these instances, as they make sure to clearly identify where information is coming from and whether it has been verified, tacitly asking the audience to weigh in and judge for themselves whether it can be trusted.

## Notes

1 Chowdhury's essay won the 2020 Dalton Camp Award, a national competition that asks writers to make a link between democracy and the media in Canada.
2 This law, Bill 21, which came into effect in March 2019, bans the wearing of religious symbols, including headscarves, by people working in the public service in the province of Quebec.

# 4 Diversity

In May 2020, a few months after much of Canada shut down due to the Covid-19 pandemic, a young journalist named Mackenzie Casalino tweeted this call-out: "Are you a young journalist in Canada? @kc_hoard and I have started a group chat via Facebook to keep us feeling connected. Slide into my DMs (direct messages) fellow youth if you would like to join" (Casalino, 2020). Freelance opportunities, internships, and jobs, especially for people trying to break into the industry, had been drying up and disappearing since the lockdown began in March, so the group used the chat to offer each other support. Out of this came an idea: Since they had time on their hands, why not start their own publication? Shortly after, *The Pigeon* was born, an online news start-up featuring in-depth stories written by young and inexperienced journalists from coast to coast (Griffin, 2020). To fund their venture, they turned to Patreon, asking people to support them on a monthly basis with whatever they could afford. One of their goals is to promote diversity. As their editorial board wrote, they want to prioritize "stories from Black journalists, Indigenous journalists, journalists of colour, and LGBTQ2S+ journalists" (*The Pigeon*, n.d., para 4). The idea is to provide a platform for marginalized voices to thrive, both through the journalists they publish and the stories they tell. As the editorial board put it: "Our staff of young Canadian journalists is devoted to sharing unique stories and prioritizing marginalized voices. We want to hear from underrepresented, inexperienced, and overenthusiastic journalists across Canada" (*The Pigeon*, n.d., para 2).

This chapter focuses on how crowdfunding is being used to increase the diversity of voices in journalism. It examines how journalists and would-be journalists are crowdfunding to tell stories they do not see reflected in legacy media and to create publications, such as *The Pigeon*, that focus on diversifying storytelling. As examples of this, this chapter looks at how journalists are crowdfunding to cover local news in areas where legacy news organizations are shrinking and how journalists are crowdfunding to create specifically feminist work, because they see large news holes where this type of serious content is lacking. This chapter also explores how journalists use crowdsourcing to try to diversify their sources and expand the range of stories they can tell.

Using the sociological concept of structuration (Giddens, 1984), which has also been used in communication and media studies to talk about hierarchies of power (Mosco, 2009), this chapter asks the reader to consider how crowdfunding journalists are attempting to exert agency in a journalism industry that is shrinking and increasingly difficult to break into. These journalists are hoping to create change with their journalism, and see themselves as working to give a voice to underrepresented people and issues. Similarly, crowdsourcing can also be seen through the lens of structuration, as journalists use this technique to diversify their sources and stories. This chapter also critically examines the limitations of this type of outreach, including the silos and hierarchies that exist in social media that can lead to certain voices being amplified more than others.

When thinking about the benefits of crowdsourcing online and the potential for diversification of journalism, it's important not to oversimplify and ignore the harsh realities of some online spaces. The Internet is not always a friendly place, and journalists who have an online presence are not immune to the hate and abuse that occurs within this space. As such, this chapter addresses the lack of civility that can arise in online spaces when the "former audience" (Gillmor, 2004) is invited to participate in the news. Journalists use a variety of tactics to deal with the abuse and threats that occur through these channels, and some journalism organizations are even shutting down comments sections because they have become too hostile.

## Opening the gates

Crowdfunding is often positioned as a way to tell stories that don't get coverage in mainstream, legacy media (Trasel & Fontoura, 2015). Even though some journalists feel a sense of discomfort in this entrepreneurial space, as discussed in Chapter 2 many do feel empowered by crowdfunding, as it gives them a chance to work outside of legacy media. It affords journalists a sense of agency, that they have power and can change, even in some small way, how journalism is done. All the journalists in this research spoke very positively about the freedom they feel crowdfunding has given them in this regard, whether it's to create one-off stories or publications devoted to independent journalism. As one journalist described:

I feel like it offers the opportunity to get the story out there that someone wouldn't report on normally. So, I feel in that way there's almost a need for it. To get other things out there that wouldn't be out there. To allow writers to go down a path where maybe at the beginning there's not as much support, or there's a more open ending to it. I feel crowdfunding provides a lot of opportunities.

(Journalist, $3,200 USD, Kickstarter)

In a similar vein, a freelance journalist who ran a Kickstarter campaign to fund a trip to Afghanistan said he wanted to cover stories he felt were not being covered accurately by Western reporters who were largely embedded with American or NATO troops:

What interests me is what is *not* being covered. Which was, and is, the perspective of the Afghan people. So, I was interested in staying and living with local people and getting a sense of the war and the occupation from their point of view.

(Journalist, $25,000 USD, Kickstarter)

## Local news

Often this interest in telling untold or overlooked stories focuses on the community level. As one journalist in the United States said, crowdfunding allowed him to tap into stories in his community that weren't being covered by legacy media, which he felt was largely driven by the daily news cycle and full of superficial coverage. His start-up was going to spend more time covering stories to bring a new depth to local reporting.

We do the kind of reporting that no one else is doing in our region. You can call it investigative. You can call it explanatory reporting. It's more in depth. It's not following the news cycle. It's data intensive, focused on public policy choices that people may or may not be talking about that are important.

($47,500 USD, Kickstarter)

Similarly, in Canada crowdfunding has been used to start publications in areas where journalists feel there is a lack of in-depth reporting. Two freelance journalists, Mathew Halliday and Chelsea Murray, raised just over $19,000 (CAD) on Kickstarter to start an online magazine devoted to covering stories in an in-depth way about Atlantic Canada. In their campaign they noted that other places in the world have successful publications devoted to long-form, in-depth journalism: "After all, Texas has *Texas Monthly*. Toronto has *Toronto Life*. California has *California Sunday*. New York has *The New York Times Magazine* (and a half-dozen others)" (The Coast, 2017, para 14). But in their area of the world there was nothing comparable. This publication, which they called *The Deep*, would "tell stories that would otherwise be unheard, in a form that illuminates them as fully, compellingly, and, yes, *deeply* as possibly" (The Coast, 2017, para 17).

Some are also crowdfunding to create news outlets where legacy media has simply disappeared. As discussed in previous chapters, after the recession of 2008 there were many cutbacks and closures in the North American journalism industry. It's a similar story today, as we live through the Covid-19 pandemic. Smaller news outlets have been among the hardest hit. For example, in March 2020, the company 22nd Century Media closed, citing financial problems due to Covid-19. The closure meant the end of 14 local newspapers around the urban Chicago area in the United States (Feder, 2020). In response, three people who used to be editors with the organization launched a Kickstarter campaign they called "The return of local news to the North Shore of Chicago" (Coughlin, 2020). They raised over $50,000 (USD) to start a nonprofit digital newsroom that will focus on news from the community, to try to bring back what had been lost. As they put it, their news organization will be "dedicated to producing credible, courageous, community-first journalism through a variety of platforms, including a daily website and weekly newsletters and podcasts" (Coughlin, 2020, para 1). But aside from larger projects to create ongoing local coverage through magazines and news start-ups, there are also campaigns to fund smaller pieces of freelance journalism focused on telling untold stories from different regions. For example, freelance journalist Thomas Crone raised just over $2,000 (USD) to tell stories about graffiti in St. Louis. Not a significant amount perhaps, compared to what has been raised for some journalism start-ups, but enough to cover costs and ensure some form of revenue (Crone, 2013).

The journalists who are crowdfunding to create local news feel strongly that it is vital their communities aren't forgotten or overlooked. Sometimes this takes the form of covering local politics and policymakers. Joey Coleman, for example, has run multiple crowdfunding campaigns in his hometown of Hamilton, Ontario in Canada, to support his publication, *The Public Record*, that focuses on coverage of local government. The publication's mission is "to provide informed coverage of Hamilton's communities and civic affairs to enable all residents to fulfill the responsibilities of citizenship by ensuring a more transparent, good civic government that is accountable to all residents of Hamilton" (Public Record, n.d., para 1).

It is significant that crowdfunding journalists are using this means to try to resurrect or create local news, for as Firmstone (2016) writes, local news is "vital to the functioning of local communities and the engagement of citizens in local democracies" (p. 928). This includes journalists interested in covering local governments, but also journalists who are interested in covering art, culture, and long-form feature journalism that is not tied to the local daily news cycle. While reporting on things like local sports teams or social events might be dismissed as gossipy or trivial, as Kleis Nielsen (2015) argues, this type of reporting can actually play an important role in building community:

> Local media help "orient" us towards each other within a shared geography, they mark the weddings, anniversaries, and funerals of those around us as relevant; they provide a common set of references that goes beyond news to include social events, sports, and the offers of local businesses.
>
> (p. 16)

In short, local journalism can help foster a sense of belonging and connection (Kim & Ball-Rokeach, 2006).

## Feminist journalism

Another notable trend on crowdfunding platforms is a wave of people who are crowdfunding to create specifically feminist content (Hunter & Di Bartolomeo, 2018). Sometimes these are freelancers who want to cover single stories that challenge stereotypical portrayals of so-called "women's issues," other times they are fundraising to create their own online magazines. For example, in her crowdfunding campaign on Kickstarter that raised just over $15,000 (USD), Kristina Kovacevic said she wanted to create a magazine for women that would cover more serious issues. She was tired of magazines aimed at women that focused on superficial things, like fashion and celebrities (Hunter & Di Bartolomeo, 2018). In her pitch to potential funders, she focused on the need to support something different:

> We'll cover news and events around the world that are important to women—inspirational, thought-provoking or stirring. You'll leave RUBY feeling smart and in the know. Health coverage will have a focus on wellness; no fad diets that help perpetuate

harmful body image stereotypes. Features that make every woman feel valued; stories about girls who are changing the world. Notably absent from our feature lineup will be any kind of gossip. We won't sensationalize. Any kind of celebrity coverage will be reserved for women who are employing their fame for the greater good. We will not promote materialistic, unattainable celebrity culture.

(Kovacevic, 2015, paras 10–12)

Often these crowdfunding campaigns focus specifically on diversity. For example, *Ladybeard* magazine from Cambridge, UK raised over £4,000 (GBP) to create a student-run feminist magazine. On their website they described themselves as more inclusive than mainstream media. "We platform the voices that you won't hear in women's magazines; voices of people who live any and every deviation from the straight, white, cis, able-bodied 'ideal'" (Hunter & Di Bartolomeo, 2018, p. 11). Similarly, the website Femsplain that raised over $30,000 (USD) on Kickstarter said in their campaign they wanted to curate content that "challenged the way the world saw us" (Gordon, 2015, para 9). Diversity was also key to their campaign and their reason for creating the online platform:

We're a diverse collective (sexuality, racial, economic, career, geographical, etc.) of doers who have made it our mission to change the dialogue of what it's like to be a woman—and in doing so, make our world a better place.

(Gordon, 2015, para 6)

It's clear when looking closely at these campaigns, and others like them, that they are taking on mainstream, so-called "women's magazines" that focus on fashion, celebrities, relationship advice, and, inevitably, body image ideals masquerading as healthy living. Much of the focus of these mainstream magazines is on selling products, rather than focusing on ideas. The people who are crowdfunding to create feminist content are trying to change how women are portrayed in the media and bring diverse perspectives into a media ecosystem that has portrayed women narrowly and superficially, within a capitalist system. By doing so they can be seen as exerting agency in a media industry that is difficult to gain access to, and trying to publish stories and issues that do not get coverage in legacy media (Hunter & Di Bartolomeo, 2018).

## Structuration and agency

These crowdfunding campaigns that are attempting to diversify the media landscape, whether by covering local news or creating feminist content, can be contextualized using the theory of structuration, a sociological concept (Giddens, 1984) that is also used in political economic theory (Mosco, 2009). Broadly, a political economic approach is interested in who has power and who doesn't. It doesn't take capitalism as a given, as something that is natural or normal, rather it questions how such a system was built, who it helps and who it doesn't. Structuration asks us to consider the give and take between social structures and individuals. Social structures refer to social norms, traditions, and moral codes. You can think of these structures in larger terms—how the wider society you live in regulates itself, but you can also think about this on a smaller level, how your own family or group of friends develops traditions and social norms that you are expected to adhere to. The point is, we are all constrained and enabled by these structures. At the same time though, these structures aren't static. As individuals, we can, to varying degrees, exert agency and influence over these structures and create change. The theory of structuration unites the ideas of structure and agency to look at how social systems are produced and reproduced. In other words, although individuals have agency, we all live within certain social structures (norms, traditions, moral codes). At the same time, we construct or reproduce these social structures, which also means we can change them. Some, however, have more power to create change than others.

In the context of crowdfunding, when we use a political economic lens to understand what is occurring, structuration can be used to look at how journalists are raising money so they can operate outside of legacy media structures, interact with them on their own terms if they are freelancers, or build entirely new media structures. It can be used to think about how much agency journalists have, or don't have, as they try to challenge the system in place. In a media ecosystem that is financially stretched, and where closures and cutbacks are becoming more and more prevalent, people who are crowdfunding to create journalism in order to fill a void or create change can be seen as exerting agency. As Tegwyn Hughes, the managing editor of *The Pigeon*, said, crowdfunding allows journalists to operate independently, as the only investors they're indebted to are their readers. As she described, crowdfunding is enabling the young and inexperienced journalists she's working with to start something new:

It's kind of a great equalizer crowdfunding, because you don't have to have some major connections in Torstar or Canadian Press to get an investor. You don't need to go to lunches and woo anybody, you just need to do good work and people will see that work and recognize that financially if they can and I think that's a really cool way to go about things.

Giddens (1984) cautions that the idea of agency implies that there is action, and that one should not conflate intention with agency. Wanting to change something and actually making change are two very different things (Parker, 2000). This is further complicated in that structural change can be hard to measure. In the examples highlighted in this chapter, intention and action are intertwined. These journalists may not be making huge waves in the media landscape, but small change counts for something, and each of the examples in this chapter show how journalists and would-be journalists are not only advocating for change by trying to diversify the range of voices that are heard in the media landscape, but by using the tools of crowdfunding to try to make this happen, even if it is on a small scale. Hughes, for example, said *The Pigeon* was born, in part, because "of students feeling really frustrated with the stifling of marginalized voices through established journalism" and they are hoping their publication will be one step towards rectifying this. As will be explored in the next chapter, one way they are doing this is by explicitly allocating part of their funds to supporting marginalized contributors.

## Crowdsourcing

The theory of structuration can also be used to contextualize what is happening with crowdsourcing in journalism. Journalists are using crowdsourcing to diversify the voices they hear from and reach a broader range of sources. By reporting stories that reach out to a larger range of people they are actively trying to change the narratives in media, and create change in the overall media structure, opening up the range of experience we have access to as media consumers. As discussed in Chapter 1, journalists are encouraged to foster a wide circle of friends and acquaintances. The idea being the wider your circle, the more diverse your stories will be. As one senior journalist said, social media call-outs can be a useful way to diversify your sources and bring people into stories who you may not otherwise have connected with through your offline social groups. As she said, "I'm mindful of wanting to make sure there is a diversity of voices and that people have a chance and opportunity in this media environment to share their experiences." She says Twitter can be a good tool to spread your call-out beyond your networks, especially when people retweet you. While she often will start with trying to connect with sources through people she knows offline and has tangible connections with, she says social media has been useful to connect her with people not in her immediate sphere who may not realize they have a story that is of interest to mainstream media. As she described, turning to social media can help connect you with people who "would not have seen or even thought about the value of their experience or their views being of worth to a mainstream media publication."

One early-career journalist who has a limited following on Twitter said he has had more success using Facebook to crowdsource, because he finds you can be more targeted in who you are trying to reach. It is easier for him to access communities he is not part of through these groups, rather than putting out a wide call on Twitter that may not reach the people he's looking for:

> Facebook I think is a lot better because you can be a lot more specific in who you are reaching out to. There are very clearly defined communities there. You can post within groups that only include people within a certain neighbourhood. Facebook, I think, has the advantage of allowing a journalist to enter communities that they are not necessarily integrated in and put out their net in those places.

Another early-career journalist who works in daily news said she uses Facebook and Twitter on a regular basis to reach out to people. She doesn't use it for experts, as she has a database compiled that she usually calls on, but if she's looking for someone affected by a story, she will turn to social media to gather the "everyday voice." As she said, especially during the Covid-19 pandemic, where she does not go out as much to get reactions to news stories from people on the street or approach people at the scene of stories, social media has helped her diversify her sources: "It has helped me step out of my usual contacts and diversify the sources that I approach and it helps me get those everyday voices." Another journalist said social media has helped him reach communities he's not part of offline: "A lot of my connections to the Muslim community are from social media. A lot of connections to the Indigenous community are through social media."

What these journalists are doing when they reach out to potential new sources on social media can be thought of in terms of Granovetter's

(1973) theory of the strength of weak ties. According to this theory, the relationships we have include both strong and weak ties. Our strong ties are close friends and family who we know very well. Our weak ties are the people we are not necessarily very close to, but think of as friends or acquaintances, or people we know tangentially through others. These weak ties may be linked to our strong ties, but we don't share the same strong bonds with them. Granovetter's theory posits that opportunities, such as job opportunities or other useful leads, are more likely to come from these weak ties. This is their strength. Since we're so close to our strong ties and we generally have fewer of them, it's unlikely we're going to get many new leads or opportunities directly from them. But our weak ties, who have their own circles of strong and weak ties they can tap into, can be valuable sources of new information. The crux of this theory is the more weak ties you have, the more opportunities may come your way. For journalists who crowdsource through social media, their weak ties are the followers they may not know or be close to offline. The more followers they have, the more opportunities for reaching sources. And of course, their followers will also have followers that journalists can reach if their tweets are retweeted, or call-outs shared on other social media. Granovetter's theory is likely implicitly understood by anyone who is concerned with networking, and certainly it's a concept that's talked about a lot in business circles (Guillory, 2019). However, there are limitations to how this idea works in online spaces. First, it has to be acknowledged that not everyone lives online. One senior journalist, who said that doing story call-outs on social media has helped her "cast the net a bit wider," also cautioned that these sorts of call-outs are "still within the umbrella of Twitter and social media and we know as journalists that it is only a small segment of society that spends their time on a platform like this." She made the point that if a journalist truly wants to be diverse in their storytelling, they need to consider offline spaces as well. Second, for those who are connected, the Internet is not a place where all voices are given equal amplification. While research has found that Twitter can amplify voices which are not part of mainstream media, significantly shifting the traditional "gatekeeper" role of legacy journalism (Hermida, 2017), others argue that it can also be a place that mimics offline life, where certain voices are given more power and distributed more widely than others. A-listers whose voices are heard offline, are often A-listers whose voices are amplified online (Haas, 2005). As an example of this, one early-career journalist I spoke to said that he has not had much luck on Twitter, because he only has 500 followers and his reach is limited. However, his tweets get a lot more traction when the news organization he works for retweets him. This organization is a major player in the Canadian journalism industry and has almost a million followers.

Many journalists are also aware they may be operating in "silos" online that will hinder their reach. The Internet has been likened to an echo-chamber where it's possible to only come into contact with people who think like us (Hassan, 2008; Sunstein, 2007). This can be through choice, who you choose to follow and friend on social media. But it is also a system that perpetuates itself. Once you start "liking" or "following" certain people or ideas on social media, the algorithms behind these social media machines start to show you content that is similar to what you have "liked" before, creating "filter bubbles" (Pariser, 2011) that can end up restricting what you see.

As Carlson (2017) writes, the concern is that this can restrict the range of news and voices that people have access to:

> In making invisible decisions about content these filters can reinforce existing interests and beliefs by feeding more of this content while omitting other news or viewpoints deemed to be a poor match. On an individual level, filter bubbles reduce exposure to a wider range of topics. From a social level, the fear is that such filters reduce the spread of news stories or topics of importance to a wide audience.
>
> (pp. 227–228)

It often has to be a deliberate decision to go out and start searching for ideas or opinions that differ from your own. In crowdsourcing, while social media circles will give journalists access to people who hold similar values, it will not necessarily reach a wide range of sources, unless journalists make conscious decisions to widen their contacts, or as some journalists do, go searching for specific groups on platforms like Facebook.

When journalists don't reach the sources they are looking for online, they do turn to more traditional methods of offline crowdsourcing. For example, when ProPublica and NPR joined forces to investigate maternal deaths and health-related complications in the United States, even though they were overwhelmed with responses, they noticed a hole. There were 2,500 stories that came in during the first week, but of those less than 75 came from Black mothers. They had the statistics that said Black mothers are three to four times more likely to die than white mothers, so they realized they would have to "devote special attention to reaching the black community" (Gallardo, 2018, para 12). To do this, they didn't count on the Internet. Instead, they used flyers and did presentations in person to "spread the word among black-serving maternal groups and at gatherings of women of color" (Gallardo, 2018, para 12).

## Audiences and civility

At the same time that audience engagement is encouraged by media outlets and journalists and seen as something potentially positive, it has to be acknowledged that engaging with the public is not always a good experience. The feedback journalists get on Twitter can be characterised by hate and abuse. Journalists who are Black, Indigenous, and people of colour are regularly subjected to racist attacks online. Female journalists are subjected to misogynist attacks, ranging from insults targeting their looks and intelligence, to unwanted sexual advances, to threats of violence (Duffy, 2019; Duncan, 2020; Knight, 2018; Westcott, 2019). A 2018 survey of female journalists from around the world (almost 600 people responded) found that "nearly 2 out of 3 respondents said they'd been threatened or harassed online at least once" (Ferrier, 2018, p. 7). Journalists use different strategies to deal with the abuse. One female senior journalist said she is open to hearing other points of view, but she uses the mute button to silence anyone who is being abusive:

> I do use my mute button from time to time, but only on people that I think are not interested in engaging or saying anything valid. I'm not interested in using the mute button to block out differing points of view. I think it's good for me to see and hear. I think it's good for all of us to see and hear other points of view that are not ours. But if they're just being downright abusive I will mute them.

This journalist said that because she is a print journalist, she doesn't face the same amount of abuse that female television journalists do, attacks that target their physical appearance or how their voices sound. Katie Simpson, a reporter in Washington for the CBC who appears regularly on television, wrote the following on Twitter:

> I dread looking at my phone due to high volume of angry content that is typically not related to my journalism. Open to suggestions on ways to reduce receiving such content, and ways to support other journalists going through same.
>
> (Simpson, 2020)

In response, Althia Raj, a journalist with the Huffington Post, said that blocking was the way to go. "It's the only way to keep sane. I used to mute but now block, block, block. And I report the really offensive things sent to me via DM" (Raj, 2020).

The Committee to Protect Journalists recommends that journalists set up separate work and personal phone, email and social media accounts, and make sure the information about them online is limited, including asking friends and family not to post personal information (Committee to Protect Journalists, 2019). However, even if a journalist takes precautions, sometimes people do find their information. For instance, one senior journalist said that she is not sure how someone found her address, as she is very careful with what she puts online, yet somehow it was dug up:

> They found my address online and tweeted it to whoever was following them. I did complain about that to Twitter. Luckily it turned into nothing. It actually wasn't my address anymore, but a loved one was living there. So scary stuff like that does happen.

Another early-career journalist cautioned that you need to be very careful about putting your personal information online, but at the same time said it is difficult to decide what to hold back, because journalists have better success if they appear to be a "real person" on their social media profiles. Sources are more willing to talk to them if they see they have friends and a life on social media.

> I would say you're more likely to have success interacting with someone if they can go on your profile and see you're a real person with real friends, but the thing that you're doing though in that situation is inviting them into your very real, everyday life. You're giving them a direct line for communication that is shared with my family and my friends.

How much information to put online and how much to keep offline is also a difficult line to negotiate when you are expected to be active on social media by your employer. One early-career journalist said that her company encourages her to promote herself as a "brand" on social media, but she is reluctant to do so. She is very careful about what she puts online, keeping her personal life and her personal opinions to herself. For her this is the safe approach, but she does wonder if it inhibits her reach:

I tend to be a very closed off person online. And I don't know if that's to my detriment ... I don't know again if that harms me in my potential to connect with new people, but I find it's a safe way for me to go about my job.

She has a private Instagram, open only to friends she knows offline, but on her other online platforms she is "strictly business."

Another mid-career journalist said that he is careful to not put identifying information about his family members online, but he is very open about his personal life and opinions. He said it has helped him in his reporting:

What I've learned about relating to people and making people comfortable is to be an open book ... I want to be as sincere as I can and as open as I can, as I expect that from people for my work. I would feel as though it's unfair to ask people to bear their heart to me and to give me their most difficult stories without at the very least being open (myself).

However, he is cognizant that as a cis white, straight male, he is in a position of privilege and what he is comfortable putting online is very much affected by this identity. He said he has had threats of physical harm from people who disagree with his opinions or his reporting, but said the type of abuse he receives online is nothing compared to journalists he knows who are women, especially Black women and women of colour. "What I experience is not fun, but what they experience is much worse."

When journalists do decide to step back from social media in the face of abuse, it can be isolating. As Heather Mallick, a Canadian print reporter, has said, she's had to retreat from engaging the public, both online and offline:

I went on Twitter, I think in 2011 and that turned horrible fairly quickly. I'm isolated now. I no longer tweet on Twitter, I just retweet. I don't answer my phone in the newsroom, because it's the same guys yelling at me all the time and leaving messages. I absolutely will not open mail unless it's from a company I recognize sending me a book.

(Mallick, 2017)

One female mid-career sports journalist who has experienced a lot of abuse online, including rape threats, said it is very difficult to deal with, but she refuses to be "quiet" on social media:

I just always think they're jealous. They wish they were doing what I was doing and they're trying to make me shut up. So, if I shut up it's kind of like I let the terrorists win. So that's why I just talk louder.

She says it's necessary for her to be on Twitter for her work, so logging off is not an option. She blocks and ignores people online who are abusive, and has also gone to the police. She said not much has come of it, but she wants the abuse to be "on the record." She said to deal with the pressure she makes sure to surround herself with encouraging people in her offline life. One early-career journalist, who is part of a collective putting out an online publication they are crowdfunding to support, said that it helps being part of a group. They said it's harder to deal with the hate and abuse that can happen online as a freelancer, but it is a bit easier if you're working with a group of people who understand what you are going through. "It's really nice to even just have a group of people that you know are supporting you or who are willing to talk to you about it who understand the situation."

Some journalism organizations have stopped allowing comments on stories where they predict the backlash is going to be racist and abusive. For example, several news sites in Canada, including the CBC, have restricted or banned comments on stories about Indigenous people (Gerster, 2020). Brodie Fenlon, the Acting Director of Digital News at the time, wrote that the CBC feels strongly about the importance of comments sections, that it helps the public broadcaster fulfil its mandate "to reflect the country and its regions to itself" (Fenlon, 2015, para 8). The comments section on stories, he wrote, "provide the public with a democratic space where they can freely engage and debate the issues of the day" (para 8). However, despite what the comment section can facilitate in terms of engaging the public in debate, the level of hate and vitriol on Indigenous stories was unacceptable:

> We've noticed over many months that these stories draw a dis-proportionate number of comments that cross the line and violate our guidelines. Some of the violations are obvious, some not so obvious; some comments are clearly hateful and vitriolic, some are simply ignorant. And some appear to be hate disguised as ignor-ance (i.e., racist sentiments expressed in benign language).
>
> (para 14)

Similarly, when *Vice News* decided to stop allowing comments in 2016, then Editor-in-Chief Johnathan Smith, prefaced the move by acknowledging that comments sections can be really valuable. As he put it: "At their best, comments can foster a productive community discussion around a particular story or topic, often providing insight or commentary that might have been missed otherwise" (Smith, 2016, para 2). However, if they are not watched closely, they can quickly devolve:

> Without moderators or fancy algorithms, they are prone to anarchy. Too often they devolve into racist, misogynistic maelstroms where the loudest, most offensive, and stupidest opinions get pushed to the top and the more reasoned responses drowned out in the noise.
>
> (para 3)

## Conclusions

Crowdfunding and crowdsourcing are used by journalists to try to diversify the media landscape. Crowdfunding journalists are raising money to report on stories they don't see reflected in legacy media, or start up entire platforms to focus on underreported stories. Similarly, crowdsourcing journalists are using social media to reach out to a wider range of sources and diversify their storytelling. This can be contextualized using the sociological theory of structuration, in that they are using these tools to try to create change in the journalism landscape. This chapter makes the argument that even if these journalists are not making large waves, the effort they are putting in and small changes they are making are worthwhile. That said, there are limitations to these practices and they are also being used to replicate existing legacy media models. While some journalists and journalism organizations are using crowdfunding so they don't have to rely on corporate support, as discussed in Chapter 2, many journalists who are starting their own media platforms are hoping to eventually move into an advertising model. So, while crowdfunding can be positioned as a tool that lets journalists operate outside legacy media, it needs to be acknowledged that it is also being used as a stepping stone to reproduce ways in which legacy media operate. As discussed in this chapter, while social media is a valuable tool journalists use to expand their reach, it can be difficult to break free of online "silos." It is also a place where many journalists face abuse and harassment. Someone outside of journalism might ask, why not shut down your social media accounts and step away from it? The short answer: it's not an easy thing for journalists to do. As one journalist said: "Being on Twitter is so vital for journalists in so many ways." It's become an important place for journalists to connect with sources, showcase their work, and create their brands. As Kat Duncan (2020), from the Missouri School of Journalism, writes:

> Online harassment can occur without warning. It can be about a tweet you sent, a story you published or a comment you responded to. But journalists cannot shut down their Facebook, Twitter and email. We have to be accessible to the public, which means we are accessible to constant abuse, harassment and personal attacks as well.
>
> (para 1)

While there are some journalists who do shut down their social media accounts or step away for certain periods of time, it is rare. Participating in social media is simply seen as part of the job and non-negotiable.

# 5 Best practices

## Introduction

As crowdfunding and crowdsourcing journalists adopt these practices, they are negotiating and redefining the boundaries of the profession. This chapter looks at best practices, identifies areas where these models may not work as well, and situations where journalists are still figuring out how they want to use them, which can differ from person to person. Turning first to crowdfunding, the chapter looks at issues of agency, both for journalists and audiences, and how the promises of crowdfunding are tempered by the work involved. Crowdfunding is also not a sure-thing, especially on platforms like Kickstarter that are "all-or-nothing"—if you make the goal you set, you get the funding, but if you come in under, you don't get any of the money that was pledged. The idea here is this policy protects donors' investments, as creators are more likely to go through with the project that was pitched if they have the full amount (Kickstarter, n.d.b). In terms of best practices that are being developed, this section deals first with issues of transparency and how journalists might consider incorporating this into their crowdfunding design. This includes transparency around how money will be spent, the role funders will play, and how journalists approach their reporting. The second theme—diversify—focuses on workload and long-term survival, including assembling a team with varied expertise and diversifying your revenue stream.

This chapter will then turn to crowdsourcing. It will reinforce some of the main points of this book, that crowdsourcing can be a useful tool to help journalists diversify their sources that has been ingrained as part of journalists' everyday work lives. However, crowdsourcing can also be time-consuming and blur the work/home boundary. It is also easy to be trapped in "silos" online, which can limit a journalist's reach. Looking at best practices, this chapter will also address the theme of transparency, but in this case how it relates to identifying crowdsourced material and how journalists negotiate transparency about their personal lives online. The second theme—choice—will look at how choice of platform and choice of question can help or hinder a journalist's efforts. Finally, this section will address the digital divide. While this might not seem as great a concern as it would have been a decade or two ago, the reality is there are people who are not online. This chapter concludes by looking at two threads that run through all this research: a commitment to public service and community. Journalists are using these tools because they believe in journalism as a public good that serves a vital role in informing and strengthening community.

## Crowdfunding

Crowdfunding enables journalists and would-be journalists to create content outside the confines of legacy media, and to cover stories they feel are important that have been missed or underreported in mainstream coverage. However, the decision to crowdfund is more than simply a response to issues they have with what is covered—or not—in legacy media, it is a way to create jobs in journalism at a time when full-time work is scarce and freelance budgets are drying up. Many journalists turn to crowdfunding precisely because it enables them to create jobs outside legacy media and typical funding structures, and get started in a business where there are not many job opportunities. For example, the Canadian online magazine *The Pigeon* was started by young and inexperienced journalists because, as their managing editor Tegwyn Hughes said, "the amount of opportunities and the compensation for those opportunities is fairly slim." While some of their contributors and members have jobs in the industry, Hughes said that "many of us were unable to find any or were really just overwhelmed," so they decided to start something themselves. For those who object to commercialization of news, and worry that news is being affected or directed by advertising dollars, this was a way to create something that gets away from this. As this journalist, who raised money for an online magazine, said:

> We really thought that it was an innovative, creative, responsible and sustainable way of funding journalism. It really got around some of the key objections that we had about journalism funding in the first place. It was outside of the commercial structured way of doing business.
>
> ($19,000 USD, Kickstarter)

This journalist also liked crowdfunding, because he said it allowed the audience to be "active." Crowdfunding is often positioned as empowering for audiences; instead of sitting back and passively consuming news that is offered to them, they can actively shape the news by putting their money behind ventures and stories they feel are important.

That said, as this book has shown, crowdfunding is also a lot of work. The creation of crowdfunding campaigns requires careful thought and planning. It requires people who have diversified skills, including writing, video production, and financial planning. For journalists running one-off crowdfunding campaigns, once the campaign is planned, the work is just beginning. For the duration of the campaign journalists have to focus on publicity, reaching out to potential donors through social media and personal contacts. As mentioned earlier, all journalists said this was incredibly time-consuming, with one journalist who was raising money for an online new site describing it point blank as a "second full-time job" ($47,500 USD, Kickstarter). It's also a type of work that can be difficult for those who are not used to thinking about the financial side of journalism. Especially for journalists who come from legacy media, the idea of asking for money and trying to market what they are doing felt foreign. For these reasons, if one is going to take this on, it is important to consider putting together a diverse team that has skills that reach into all these areas. There were some journalists who ran campaigns over and over again, but they were rare. Most tried once and that was enough.

Crowdfunding is also not a sure thing. According to Kickstarter's latest statistics, only 22.81% of journalism campaigns are fully funded (Kickstarter, n.d.a). As well, there is a cost to crowdfunding on these platforms. On Kickstarter you don't get charged if you don't make your goal, but if you do the company takes 5%, plus processing fees which vary from country to country (usually in the range of 3–5%). On Indiegogo, the cost is 4% of a successful campaign and 9% of an unsuccessful campaign. (Unlike Kickstarter's all-or-nothing policy, on Indiegogo you can collect money if you only partially meet your goal.) If crowdfunding is part of a larger organization's financial planning there needs to be people dedicated to running this aspect of the business, which of course takes up resources.

## Best practices: transparency

### *Follow the money*

For crowdfunding to be successful, it is important to have very clear goals and deliverables that can be easily conveyed to potential funders. As one journalist raising money for an online publication said:

We learned that special projects that have a begin date and end date and where you have a clear deliverable are the ones that have the most success because people know that, if nothing else, you won't forget about telling them about the outcome. You'll give the donors a sense of completion and follow through.

($19,400 USD, Spot.us)

But aside from transparency with objectives and deliverables, many journalists are also focusing on transparency with their funding. This goes some way to corroborate what Singer (2015) writes, that "[t]here is some evidence that (transparency) is being called upon in ethical considerations of entrepreneurial journalism ... whether involving a commercial or a nonprofit enterprise" (p. 31). The journalists in this research focused on transparency as a key element of their pitches. Those who were crowdfunding on single platform campaigns took care to list exactly why they needed the money they were asking for and where it would be spent. It was seen as sound practice to incorporate this into a pitch so potential donors would feel confident about what they were backing. For example, Canadian freelance journalist Naheed Mustafa, in her pitch to travel to Pakistan and Afghanistan to cover stories from the region, went into detail about where the money would go, including how much would be spent on airfare, room and board, a fixer to help her arrange interviews, a translator, and drivers (Mustafa, 2013). *The Pigeon* is using Patreon to raise money and offers funders the choice of different levels of support. This is not unusual, most crowdfunding campaigns do this, but what they are doing differently is giving people the choice to specify where they would like their donation spent. First, they have a general fund that will go where the editors see the most need. Donors can also choose to have their money go into an operating fund, which will support the upkeep of the website and other technical issues related to their site operation. Or donors can choose to have their money go directly to what they call the marginalized contributor fund. All money donated to this fund "will be directly redistributed to marginalized young journalists who write for *The Pigeon*" (*The Pigeon*, n. d.). As Tegwyn Hughes said, they felt it was very important to be transparent about the different funding tiers so that donors felt confident about where their money was going. One of the stated goals of the publication is to provide a voice for marginalized contributors, and pay them when possible, so they wanted to make sure donors who wanted to support this aspect of the publication felt confident their money was being used for this purpose:

I think we're putting our money where our mouth is by being transparent about the funding that goes towards marginalized contributors. While a lot of the money that we will be getting in our general fund will be set aside for contributors I think by allowing people to donate specially to that fund we are saying that at the end of the day if we need an extra five dollars to pay for our domain, but that (extra five dollars) is in our marginalized contributor fund, we're not going to touch that money. That money is for that one goal.

Some larger organizations are also explicit about where money from supporters is going, usually specifying that it will be going directly to fund the creation of journalism and emphasizing that donors are playing a key role in making sure journalism remains open and accessible; donor contributions are keeping paywalls down and enabling the organizations to remain independent.

### *Role funders will play*

Most journalists in this study were very clear about how they stood in relationship to independence and autonomy. The reason many were crowdfunding in the first place was to ensure they could remain independent. They saw crowdfunding as a way to break free from any sort of obligation to advertisers or corporate ownership. However, this does raise questions about the responsibility journalists feel towards the people who are supporting them. When asked, most journalists had developed clear boundaries in their thinking about this: while they valued their donors and respected their opinions, to the point where they would go to them for story ideas or suggestions, they drew the line at editorial interference. It's complicated though, because they developed strong feelings of gratitude and a sense of responsibility. One journalist who was raising money for an online magazine said they were "genuinely curious" to see what kind of stories people would want to see in their crowdsourced magazine:

> These people are (the) most passionate, most devoted initial audience so of course we want to know what they think so we can tailor it to some degree. There is a sense of responsibility to think about what kind of magazine we can produce that will be what they're looking for.
>
> ($19,000 CAD, Kickstarter)

That said, most journalists didn't feel balancing responsibility with independence would be problematic; they didn't expect any donors to take issue with the journalism they were going to produce. Those who were crowdfunding to create advocacy journalism, and those I describe as having a "point of view," felt most donors agreed with their stance and were supporting them precisely because they wanted to see journalism that reflected this. As one journalist said, who was raising money for an online news publication, the donors weren't just investing in journalism, they were "investing in our belief system" (journalist, $300/month on Patreon).

While it was clear that journalists had thought through these ideas, very few had clearly stated in their campaigns where they stood in terms of editorial control, whether they were looking for passive or active investors, and what sort of engagement they would like from their funders—were they looking for feedback or a form of co-creation? As Aitamurto (2013) has shown, co-creation with audiences can be difficult when readers' expectations and story judgement clashes with journalists' expectations. In Aitamurto's study of the co-creation process at a magazine, readers did develop a sense of closeness with the magazine, something that crowdfunding journalists want to develop with their funders, but readers were unhappy that their input was not synthesized into the work of the journalists, rather treated as separate content. Even if they don't feel it's going to be an issue, crowdfunding journalists would be well served to clearly define what sort of relationship they want with their funders, including input into story design and development, and outline this in their initial pitches. Again, though, this is complicated, because they are trying to foster a sense of community, or sense of connection with their donors, and drawing boundaries could be seen to be at odds with this. Interestingly, to cope with this discrepancy many journalists are replicating what happens in legacy media, drawing on the metaphor of invisible walls and enforcing a separation between money and content, even if the two collapse in this kind of entrepreneurial setting.

In terms of limiting the potential for conflict of interest, taking care to know who your donors are and making sure they aren't in conflict with any stories you might be pursuing would also be a sound practice. Several journalists in this research were very cognizant of this, and took pains to make sure they set up this boundary. As well, the now defunct Spot.us model that limited investment from one particular funder to 20% of the total costs of the operation, forces a distribution of funding. Journalists who are using other crowdfunding sites might consider adopting this practice, even if it is not built into the platform.

*Point of view*

The journalists interviewed in this research were all very clear where they stood in relation to journalistic norms of impartiality, fairness, and balance. However, not everyone made this explicit on their crowdfunding campaigns. Some who came from legacy media, where these norms have been well entrenched, were carrying this over into their crowdfunding ventures. Others were openly crowdfunding to create advocacy journalism and were looking for people who agreed with them to help bring their journalism to life. More complicated and nuanced were the people I characterize as somewhere in between these two polarities, journalists with a "point of view" who felt this doesn't get in the way of reporting accurately and fairly. As one journalist said, the people they work with have similar values and this comes across in the stories they choose to cover and the sources they go to. They don't try to hide it, in fact it makes them what they are. While she doesn't shy away from the word "objectivity," she sees it as a process, rather than a goal or obligation to present different sides of a story equally:

> We try to adhere to the journalistic process and a degree of objectivity, in order for the work that we produce to not be unreasonably biased, but I think that what we come out with definitely reflects what we value and what our publication values and the content that we produce from the beginning to end will also reflect that.
>
> (Journalist, $300/month CAD, Patreon)

Another journalist, raising money for the same online news publication as the journalist above, described their approach in a similar fashion— while they have personal opinions, they can be upfront about them and still look at an issue widely:

> Yes, I have personal opinions. I'm not going to hide those personal opinions. But I'm going to try my best to be accountable to my readership and not leave things out that I think are pertinent to the story that would allow them to develop their own opinions.
>
> (Journalist, $300/month CAD, Patreon)

The comments from these journalists reflect many of the discussions going on now in social media, legacy media, and newsrooms around how norms such as objectivity, fairness, and balance should be applied, or if they even work at all (Chowdhury, 2020; Lowery, 2020; Rosenteil, 2020a, 2020b, 2020c, 2020d, 2020e, 2020f). Being transparent about where journalists stand in terms of these norms, even if they're still working it out, would be a sound practice that might even serve to attract more donors who'd appreciate this type of clarity. Journalists are already aware of the importance of transparency in their pitches when it comes to detailing where the money will go, some clarity from the start about how they are dealing with issues around balance and point of view could also be considered.

## Best practices: diversify

### The team

Crowdfunding is an enormous amount of work, and working with a team to divide up responsibilities can help. One journalist, describing the work that was going into her campaign, was worried that all the effort might not pay off:

> We're working on a video that is taking way too long to put together. It requires a very honed marketing pitch, good polished materials and then an outreach campaign. If we put forty hours or fifty hours of work into this, what are we going to get?
>
> (Journalist, $76,000 USD, Kickstarter)

But in addition to being a lot of work, which was explored in Chapter 2, crowdfunding is also a type of work that many journalists aren't used to and consequently lack experience. Moreover, it's clear that not all journalists who crowdfund are comfortable dealing with the financial and promotional side of crowdfunding. While the journalists in this research were at ease talking about the content they were going to produce, figuring out how to be entrepreneurs was often difficult. For some it was simply uncomfortable to ask for money; they felt it was unseemly, something polite people just "didn't do." As well, working so publicly, having to justify an idea before the story or the platform is produced, was a different way of working. As one journalist who was raising money for an online publication described:

> It was a lot more work than we expected to curate and run a campaign … It was a lot of blogging and coaxing and having to justify what you're doing in a very public way. Which is something that journalists aren't typically experts at or enthusiastic about.
>
> (Journalist, $19,400 USD, Spot.us)

Most of the journalists who felt uncomfortable asking for money had spent careers in legacy media, where there was a very clear divide between the money and the journalism. One younger journalist who was raising money for an online news publication wondered if the fact that the people she was working with were in a young age demographic, that has grown up on the Internet and social media, worked to their advantage:

> We're all of a certain age bracket – 18–22ish. So, we've grown up with social media and we're very familiar with it. I think because of that and because of our online literacy we know sort of know instinctively what looks professional, what looks put together, how to speak to the demographics that we want to.
>
> ($300/month CAD, Patreon)

She said they were able to make marketing and promotional decisions quickly as a team, and weren't overly concerned with "how" to do this, or even whether they should; it came naturally. However, while this journalist makes a good point, that familiarity and comfort with online spaces can work to one's advantage, there were many older journalists in this research who embraced online platforms, creating compelling and extremely successful campaigns. As well, having extensive experience and a successful track record in journalism was helpful in bringing in donations, as some journalists noted that their careers and reputation helped them market themselves.

### The revenue stream

Many journalists saw crowdfunding as an opportunity to raise start-up funds to get a project off the ground. For some, it was a way to avoid giving up control of their news start-up and not be burdened by bank loans in the long term. As one journalist who was raising money for an online magazine described:

> [One] benefit that I saw from crowdfunding was that you could raise significant money without having to sell or give away part of your project or your business. I know there are a lot of options for investors and other types of funding, but I wasn't willing to sell off any part of [publication] at this point. I do plan on turning it into—hopefully—a profitable business. In terms of taking out loans and stuff, I didn't want to have that hanging over my head at the beginning.
>
> ($15,000 USD, Kickstarter)

This journalist hoped to make money from the venture by eventually selling advertising and subscriptions; crowdfunding was just the seed money to start what they envisioned would eventually be a profitable business. Overwhelmingly, this was the message from journalists in this research—crowdfund to get a project off the ground, but don't use it to sustain your work in the long run. It's important to have a plan, from the start, about how to diversify your revenue stream. While crowdfunding can work well for journalists who have the energy to invest in the process, who have concrete, finite projects in mind, such as start-up funds or travel funds, it is not a long-term solution to the economic uncertainty facing the field. It is, however, a place where start-ups and experiments can secure initial funding, and perhaps go on to leverage further funding through traditional advertising models or philanthropic support. As Ernst Pfauth (2015) from *De Correspondent* put it, "crowdfunding can be a great kickstart for a member-based publication, but no more than that" (para 8). *The Record North Shore*, a local news site that just raised over $58,000 (USD) on Kickstarter, was already planning from the campaign stage that money raised would be start-up funds, and they would need to transition into a steadier funding stream. As they wrote:

> When we launch, our public-service journalism (breaking news, police reports, public health and safety information) will be free to read, but in order to maintain our mission in the long-term, we will ask readers to pay a modest monthly rate for full access to credible, community-first journalism on a daily website and through weekly newsletters and podcasts.
>
> (Coughlin, 2020, para 7)

That said, there were several journalists in this research who have run multiple campaigns through one-off crowdfunding platforms, but it takes time, energy, and dedication. There are also larger organizations that use ongoing crowdfunding as one part of their revenue model. *The Guardian* in the UK, *The Tyee* in Canada, and the *Texas Tribune* in the United States are just a few of the organizations that have reader support as one of their funding sources. This should not be confused with a subscription model where readers pay for access. Organizations that crowdfund leave their content, for the most part, accessible to anyone. Contributors will sometimes get exclusive content, or perhaps a small token such as a tote bag, but essentially crowdfunding is part of the organizations' plans to keep their content freely accessible.

## Crowdsourcing

Crowdsourcing can be very helpful for journalists who are trying to diversify their sources and reach out to people they wouldn't normally know through their regular channels. It has become common practice for some journalists to go to Facebook or Twitter when chasing a story. As one early-career journalist said: "It's really just an ingrained part of what we do. The same way the rolodex would have been the go-to thing or the phone book. It is part of the everyday stuff that we do." Another mid-career journalist said it also helps him file stories more quickly, because it is easy to reach people online.

> It's (social media) become a part of a journalist's life because it's become a part of everybody's life. Everybody is constantly accessible, for the most part, on their phones. I'm sometimes amazed that you leave a message for a spokesperson or you call a government office and you leave a voicemail or you leave an email and great if they get back you that day, but it could take hours. Whereas you reach out to a potential source on Facebook and they get back to you within ten seconds.

Another mid-career journalist was very blunt in his description of how social media has helped him become the journalist he is today: "I need it. I'd still be a good reporter. I'd still be a good journalist. But I wouldn't be nearly as far along in my career if it weren't for social media." He says it has helped him connect with people outside his usual circles, and create a strong sense of trust with his followers who help him enormously with his reporting, whether it be with tips, story ideas, or as sources.

However, there are limitations to the practice. Reaching out to people on social media can be time-consuming. As one mid-career journalist said, writing out your introduction, explaining who you are, why you want to talk to them, and why you are intruding in their social media space, takes longer than a phone call or in-person introduction:

> You have to be a little bit more active in explaining who you are, why you are reaching out to them, because you are disrupting their day, you are sliding into their messages and being like "hey, can I poke in here for a second and talk to you?" It's more akin to cold-calling somebody.

Aside from reaching out, responding to people can be time-consuming, especially if a call-out on social media gets a huge response. Some journalists feel an obligation to respond to everyone who reaches out to them, whether for pragmatic reasons to keep the lines of communication open, or simply to be polite out of respect for the effort it took. Journalists want to show that they are not just jumping in and out of online communities mining for stories, but have good intentions. One way to show this, and build up trust, is to be polite and respond to everyone who has taken the time to reach out. Of course, this happens off social media as well when sources reach out over the phone or email, but on social media there is often a public record of a journalist's interactions with people, which can help build their reputation as someone who is approachable and trustworthy.

Crowdfunding through social media can also blur the line between "work life" and "home life." As several journalists pointed out, social media platforms don't shut down or turn off. It can be difficult to ignore these platforms and step away from work, and on the platforms themselves it can also be difficult to separate your work and personal life. As one early-career journalist said: "Even in your personal time and on a platform that is both professional and personal you can't have that separation. You will have potential sources reaching out to you at all times."

In addition, many journalists pointed out that the Internet can be limiting in ways we may not even be consciously aware of and it's possible to get stuck in "silos" or "filter bubbles" (Pariser, 2011). It should not be taken for granted that your reach on the Internet will be widespread, as it can take a conscious effort to break out of these silos. Finally, as discussed in the previous chapter, the Internet is not always a civil place, and journalists regularly face abuse and harassment online. In the face of these opportunities and limitations, journalists are negotiating ways of working that take advantage of what these tools have to offer and mitigate the pitfalls.

## Best practices: transparency

### Sourcing

As Singer (2015) writes, transparency in journalism has been an "undervalued and even contested norm in traditional media" (p. 31), but is becoming more prominent as journalists increasingly use social media as a reporting tool. As discussed in Chapter 3, over the past decade it has become common practice for journalists to source material they are getting from social media, especially in breaking news situations when they are not able to immediately verify information themselves. It is seen as good practice to be open about where information is coming from, who supplied it, and if warranted, whether it has been independently verified. Anyone who follows journalists on Twitter will quickly see it is becoming common practice for journalists to ask people who have recorded video or pictures from breaking news—from protests to weather events—for permission to use this material in their stories. When permission is given the material will turn up in the journalist's story, clearly sourced as coming from the person who provided it on Twitter. While some argue that crowdsourcing requires a structured "call-out," rather than harvesting information from social media, the journalists in this research disagree, and see actively going to social media to look for story ideas or sources as part and parcel of what crowdsourcing entails. This type of transparency actively engages audiences in the news process. It's an encompassing and welcoming practice that serves as a reminder that journalism isn't an exclusive club that only a few can participate in—if audiences have something valuable to add, not only will it be used, but credit will be given.

### *Privacy vs. openness*

Before social media, a journalist who talked to a source could potentially never interact with them again, retreating to the privacy of their office and closing the door. But having an online presence opens up access to a journalist in a whole new way. As one early-career journalist said, "You can't disappear into the smoke, you know. You can't go back into the protection of 'I'm away from my email' or 'I'm away from my office phone.' They (the crowd) have access to you at 3am on Sunday morning because you've given them the keys to the castle." Some journalists have found it very helpful to have these kinds of platforms, embracing this type of connection wholeheartedly, saying it has helped them connect with people and find stories. Even public critiques of their work have improved their journalism. As one mid-career journalist said:

> There have been many times where I've either made a mistake or the tone of the article was wrong and people have pointed that out. My initial reaction was very defensive, but I stopped and thought about it and it made me a better person and it made me a better writer.

However, what can't be overlooked is the abuse and harassment many journalists experience online, to the point where some choose to check out of social media completely when the bad outweighs the good.

Others are very cautious about how much they reveal about themselves online, preferring to remain "strictly business" on sites that are open to everyone, and keeping any personal social media sites private. But while this approach can go some way to mitigate the vitriol that can occur online, even those journalists who keep their personal lives off-line are not immune to hateful attacks. Opting for privacy can be a difficult decision to make. Some journalists believe it is easier to connect with sources online if they are open and transparent about who they are on social media. They said it helps builds trust if people see you as a whole person, someone who is more than just a journalist. But for others, this is simply not a safe approach. There's no easy answer or right choice when negotiating the line between privacy and openness online, journalists are deciding what works for them and their comfort level. It is problematic though that some journalists feel they have to be online under these circumstances, encouraged to promote themselves and their work as a "brand." This type of pressure should not exist given the realities of what can happen online. It also needs to be recognized that while social media can be a helpful tool, it is not the only way to do journalism and not the best way in all circumstances, given the limited reach of the Internet in some cases.

## Best practices: choice

### Choose your platform

There were interesting disagreements among journalists about which platform works best for crowdsourcing and this is something for journalists to consider when deciding what to put their energy into. One journalist said that Twitter is not really set up for community engagement, and Facebook is where he turns when he wants to connect with communities he's not part of. Twitter, he thinks, is more about performance, showing people who you are and presenting a persona to the world, while Facebook is more about community. As he put it: "Twitter I feel is not based in community engagement. It's based very much in personal expression." Another early-career journalist agreeing that Twitter isn't always the best place to find specific sources, said he only uses it as a last resort, describing it as a "Hail Mary," an expression of Catholic religious origin referring to a desperate last attempt. These journalists said they prefer to turn to Facebook where they find groups of community members already engaged in talking to each other about issues important to them. Others have had luck when casting a wide net on Twitter and use it regularly, finding it helpful to expand their range of sources and quickly connect with people. Usually, these were journalists with wide followings, who had many "weak ties" (Granovetter, 1973) that helped spread their call and tap into new sources.

### Choose your question

As discussed briefly in Chapter 4, the type of question a journalist is asking can also be important when deciding which platform to use, or whether to use social media at all. As one early-career journalist said, if she is looking for people to react to a story in the news, Twitter or Facebook works well, but it's not the place she goes looking for experts. Social media is good for quickly finding "everyday" people who are affected by news stories or have strong opinions. When she's using these platforms, the question has to be a version of "how are you affected by (insert news story of the day)"? For more large-scale crowdsourcing endeavours, the Australian Broadcasting Corporation journalists who conducted an investigation into long-term care homes emphasized that choosing the right question is of prime importance. Their success, they felt, had to do with finding a topic "where the public had genuine deep knowledge or information that journalists may not have or might find hard to access" (Puccini, Prior, & Filali, 2018, para 10). As they put it, it needed to be something that many people could relate to, "a subject that affected a lot of people and that people cared about" (para 11). In other words, just as crowdfunding isn't a "build-it-and-they-will-come" endeavour, successful crowdsourcing isn't as simple as throwing a question into the ether of social media. There is thought and planning that goes into deciding the best platform to target, and the right questions to ask. To crowdsource successfully also takes careful cultivation of social media, paying attention to how diverse your followers are, and in turn how far your reach is. Some journalists take great care to develop relationships with people who follow them, whether that's through responding to people or deciding to be open about who they are online. Others, while choosing to be more reserved in their online presence, still try to be polite, act respectfully in online groups they join, and respond to people who answer their call-outs in order to build trust. All this takes careful planning and diligent follow-through.

## Limitations: digital divide

Finally, this book would be remiss if it didn't address the digital divide. What can't be overlooked is that crowdfunding and crowdsourcing only tap into people who have Internet connections (Aitamurto, 2016). While this divide is getting smaller, there are many areas of the world that are simply not connected. Even in places where the Internet is ubiquitous there are uneven levels of access. In some households every family member has their own device; in others there may be only one device that is shared by everyone. In some households, people may have the free time to answer a journalist's call-out, but others won't. If you have children that need your attention, family members to take care of, a job that requires your full attention, etc., connecting with journalists online likely won't be your first priority in the face of these more pressing responsibilities. All of this needs to be taken in consideration when taking a wide lens approach to who is able to participate in crowdfunding and crowdsourcing, particularly when making claims that crowdfunding is empowering for donors and crowdsourcing diversifies the media landscape. Certainly, it is and it does, to a certain extent, but this reach excludes people who aren't connected and those who simply don't have the time because they are busy with other aspects of their life. If journalists want to connect with sources who may not be living online, they need to think of other ways to reach out in person. The journalists in this research were very cognizant of this, recognizing that although social media is a useful tool for crowdsourcing, it is not the only one, and their online "silos" may be unwittingly restricting their reach.

## Conclusions

Two important threads run through all the conversations in this research: public service and community. It was clear that journalists think of their work as more than just a job, but as something that is making an important contribution to public life. Journalism is seen as an essential, even vital part of a functioning democracy. It is needed to hold power to account, understand what is happening in our communities, and bring people together. Journalists aren't crowdfunding just because they need a job, they believe strongly in what the profession brings to public life. Journalism is so important they take on the significant labour of crowdfunding willingly. Because there are stories that need to be told that aren't being brought to light. Because there is a need for local news, in communities where media is disappearing. Because there is a need for feminist content that doesn't pander to stereotypes and the worst of commercial culture. Because there is a need for independent journalism, free from corporate support, that makes an important contribution to the public sphere. As one journalist who was crowdfunding to support a local news magazine said, "If you can return to the sense of journalism as a public service for a community, you can invent new models and inject some more life into journalism where it's suffered most."

Journalists also take on the labour of crowdsourcing, and all the messiness it entails when public and private lives mesh online, because they are committed to diversity, reflecting communities to themselves, and finding stories that need to be told. Rather than running from the profession because of the abuse they face online, they find ways to block it out and manage it. They deal with it because they see their job as so important to a functioning democracy and local communities, that they will manage this fall-out, no matter how disturbing it is. This commitment is very much tied to the idea of public service—they negotiate the complications of leading a public life on social media, so they can perform this important service that creates a vital public good.

There is also a commitment to community that runs through both crowdfunding and crowdsourcing. The journalists who crowdfund are looking to connect with people who care about the same issues they do, whether it's independent journalism or a specific subject they feel needs wider attention. Larger organizations who are crowdfunding as part of their funding models are looking for ways to engage with audiences so they feel connected and invested. While journalists are committed to independent journalism free from influence, at the same time there is this strong need for connection and community that underlies the work they do. Not only does crowdfunding help them to access the resources they need, it opens up the journalistic process, moving away from the idea that the journalists are the only gatekeepers. As one journalist who was crowdfunding to start an online magazine said, "I don't think journalists can afford to be lone rangers, because there's not enough resources out there anymore to do the kinds of journalism that matters. I think opening it up to community accountability is a good thing." The journalists who are crowdsourcing also showed a deep commitment to strengthening community. They were turning to social media to find ways into communities they don't normally have access to. They wanted to diversify their sources, reflect communities to themselves by telling untold stories, and build trust with people so they could to tell stories that really matter.

This book has cast a critical eye on these practices, looking at labour issues, whether crowdfunding will lead to a replication of commercially funded legacy media models, and the silos that can occur online. This is not to try to dissuade anyone, on the contrary my hope is this is an opportunity to think deeply about how these practices are changing the boundaries of journalism. There is a disruption occurring in journalistic practice as journalists crowdfund and crowdsource, and while there are challenges and questions that need to be asked before blindly jumping forward, through these disruptions runs a strong thread of hope. Hope that they offer a new sense of agency and the ability to create meaningful change. It was inspiring to talk to all of these journalists who have not given up when, at times, the profession can feel like it is in serious financial trouble and resources are scarce. They are creative, adventurous, and thoughtful as they navigate new waters, and their commitment to public service and community-building is inspiring.

# References

Aitamurto, T. (2011). The impact of crowdfunding on journalism. *Journalism Practice*, 5(4), 429–445.

Aitamurto, T. (2013). Balancing between open and closed: Co-creation in magazine journalism. *Digital Journalism*, 1(2), 229–251.

Aitamurto, T. (2015). The role of crowdfunding as a business model in journalism: A five-layered model of value creation. In L. Bennett, B. Chin, & B. Jones (Eds.), *Crowdfunding the future* (pp. 189–205). New York: Peter Lang.

Aitamurto, T. (2016). Crowdsourcing as a knowledge-search method in digital journalism. *Digital Journalism*, 4(2), 280–297.

Allen, M., Chen, C., Churchill, L., McSwane, J. D., Miller, M., Jameel, M., & Raghavendran, B. (2020, June 21). We want to talk to people working, living and grieving on the front lines of the coronavirus: Help us report. ProPublica. www.propublica.org/getinvolved/we-want-to-talk-to-people-working-or-living-on-the-front-lines-of-coronavirus-help-us-report?token=yIzUwxhFBlPUbcgl8a MwDk7gQ6AdqbgA.

Armstrong, K. [@byKenArmstrong] (2020, February 13). *For so long, the conventional wisdom in investigative reporting was: Don't let the world know what you're working on until you publish. But as @propublica's engagement team has shown—thru one powerhouse story after another—that convention needed some serious rethinking* [Tweet]. Twitter. https://twitter.com/bykenarm strong/status/1228018521184931840.

Bannerman, S. (2013). Crowdfunding culture. *Wi: Journal of Mobile Media*, 7(1). http://wi.mobilities.ca/crowdfunding-culture/.

Belleflamme, P., Lambert, T., & Schwienbacher, A. (2014). Crowdfunding: Tapping the right crowd. *Journal of Business Venturing*, 29, 585–609.

Blue, E. (2012). Taking the lane: A feminist bike zine. Kickstarter. www.kicksta rter.com/projects/ellyblue/taking-the-lane-a-feminist-bike-zine.

Bradshaw, P., & Brightwell, A. (2012). Crowdsourcing investigative journalism: Help me investigate – a case study. In E. Siapera & A. Veglis (Eds.), *The handbook of global online journalism* (pp. 251–271). West Sussex: Wiley.

Bunz, M. (2010, March 10). Time for a press award for crowdsourced journalism? *Guardian*. www.theguardian.com/media/pda/2010/mar/30/digital-m edia-crowdsourcing-crowd-sourced-journalism.

Calcutt, A., & Hammond, P. (2011). *Journalism studies*. London: Routledge.

Caraway, B. (2011). Audience labor in the new media environment: A Marxian revisiting of the audience commodity. *Media, Culture & Society*, 33(5), 693–708.

Carlson, M. (2017). Automated journalism: A posthuman future for digital news? In B. Franklin & S. A. Eldridge II (Eds.), *The Routledge companion to digital journalism studies* (pp. 226–233). New York: Routledge.

Carlson, M., & Lewis, S. C. (2015). *Boundaries of journalism: Professionalism, practice and participation*. New York: Routledge.

Carvajal, M., García-Avilés, J. A., & González, J. L. (2012). Crowdfunding and non-profit media. *Journalism Practice*, 6(5–6), 638–647.

Casalino, M. [@mmrcasalino] (2020, May 21). *Are you a young journalist in Canada? @kc_hoard and I have started a group chat via Facebook to keep us feeling connected. Slide into my DMs fellow youth if you would like to join* [*Tweet*]. Twitter. https://twitter.com/mmrcasalino/status/1263530140300185601.

Chowdhury, R. (2020, July 11). The forever battle of a journalist of colour: Dalton Camp Award winning essay. *The Star*. www.thestar.com/opinion/con tributors/2020/07/11/the-forever-battle-of-a-journalist-of-colour-dalton-camp-a ward-winning-essay.html.

CNN (2020). Hurricane Sandy fast facts. www.cnn.com/2013/07/13/world/am ericas/hurricane-sandy-fast-facts/index.html.

The Coast (2017). The Deep: Atlantic Canada's long-form magazine. Kickstarter. www.kickstarter.com/projects/415566154/the-deep-atlantic-canadas-long-form-magazine.

Coddington, M. (2015). The wall becomes a curtain: Revisiting journalism's news-advertising boundary. In M.Carlson & S. C. Lewis (Eds.), *Boundaries of journalism* (pp. 67–82). London: Routledge.

Cohen, N. (2012). Cultural work as a site of struggle: Freelancers and exploitation. *Triple C*, 10(2), 141–155.

Cohen, N. (2016). *Writers' rights: Freelance journalism in a digital age*. Montreal: McGill-Queen's University Press.

Committee to Protect Journalists (2019, September 4). Digital safety: Remove personal data from the internet. https://cpj.org/2019/09-digital-safety-rem ove-personal-data-internet/.

Condon, S. (2017, April 14). Kickstarter 101: When and how to run a crowdfunding campaign. CNET. www.cnet.com/how-to/kickstarter-101-when-a nd-how-to-run-a-successful-crowdfunding-campaign/.

Coughlin, J. (2020). The return of local news to the North Shore. Kickstarter. www.kickstarter.com/projects/therecordnews/the-return-of-local-news-to-the-no rth-shore/description.

Cox, B. (2020, April 6). Free Press employees deliver definition of dedication. *Winnipeg Free Press*. www.winnipegfreepress.com/special/coronavirus/free-p ress-employees-deliver-definition-of-dedication-569422662.html.

Crone, T. (2013). Experiential journalism. Kickstarter. www.kickstarter.com/p
rojects/nextstl/experiential-journalism-thomas-crone-and-st-louis.

Deuze, M. (2011). What is journalism? Professional identity and ideology of
journalists reconsidered. In D. Berkowitz (Ed.), *Cultural meanings of news*
(pp. 17–31). Thousand Oaks, CA: Sage.

Donnelly, A. (2020, April 6). COVID-19 crisis: Most Canadians support bailout
for media organizations, poll finds. *National Post*. https://nationalpost.com/ne
ws/canada/covid-19-crisis-most-canadians-support-bailout-for-media-organiza
tions-poll-finds.

Donsbach, W. (2012). Journalists and their professional identities. In A. Allen
(Ed.), *The Routledge companion to news and journalism* (pp. 38–48).
London: Routledge.

Duffy, C. (2019, September 8). Online harassment is the largest safety concern
for female journalists, new study finds. CNN. www.cnn.com/2019/09/08/m
edia/women-journalists-cpj-safety-survey-reliable-sources/index.html.

Duncan, K. (2020, March 24). The Cohort: Newsrooms should protect staff
against online harassment. Because they often don't, there's JSafe. Poynter.
www.poynter.org/business-work/2020/newsrooms-should-protect-staff-against-
online-harassment-because-they-often-dont-theres-jsafe/.

Elliot, J., & Eisinger, J. (2014, April 11). Long after Sandy, Red Cross post-storm
spending still a black box. ProPublica. www.propublica.org/article/long-a
fter-sandy-red-cross-post-storm-spending-still-a-black-box.

Elliot, J., Eisinger, J., & Sullivan, L. (2014, October 29). The Red Cross' secret
disaster. ProPublica. www.propublica.org/article/the-red-cross-secret-disaster.

Emery, M., & Emery, E. (1996). *The press and America: An interpretive history
of the mass media*. Boston: Allyn & Bacon.

Eng, M. (2020a, June 12). My daughter attended a protest: How do I get her
tested? WBEZ. www.wbez.org/stories/my-daughter-attended-a-protesthow-do-i-
get-her-tested/bdb8a5c7-395f-4575-b657-f47d30acd05a.

Eng, M. (2020b, June 13). Patio dining 101: Health experts weigh in on how to eat
out safely. WBEZ. www.wbez.org/stories/patio-dining-101-health-experts-
weigh-in-on-how-to-eat-out-safely/eacdbc1f-13d0-4b6d-a4c3-d7cdb204e0bd.

Engelberg, S. (2014, November 6). How crowdsourcing helped bring red cross
problems to light. ProPublica. www.propublica.org/article/how-crowdsourcin
g-helped-bring-red-cross-problems-to-light.

Feder, R. (2020, April 1). Citing coronavirus impact, 22nd Century Media goes
out of business. Robert Feder. www.robertfeder.com/2020/04/01/citing-cor
onavirus-impact-22nd-century-media-goes-business/.

Fenlon, B. (2015). Uncivil dialogue: Commenting and stories about indigenous
people. CBC News. www.cbc.ca/newsblogs/community/editorsblog/2015/11/
uncivil-dialogue-commenting-and-stories-about-indigenous-people.html.

Ferrier, M. (2018). Attacks and harassment: The impact of female journalists
and their reporting. International Women's Media Foundation. www.iwmf.
org/wp-content/uploads/2018/09/Attacks-and-Harassment.pdf.

Firmstone, J. (2016). Mapping changes in local news. *Journalism Practice*, 10(7), 928–938.

Fuchs, C. (2012). Dallas Smythe today: The audience commodity, the digital labour debate, marxist political economy and critical theory. Prolegomena to a digital labour theory of value. *Triple C*, 10(2), 692–740.

Gallardo, A. (2018, May 20). How we collected nearly 5,000 stories of maternal harm. ProPublica. www.propublica.org/article/how-we-collected-nearly-5-000-stories-of-maternal-harm.

Gasher, M., Skinner, D., & Coulter, N. (2020). *Media & communication in Canada: Networks, culture, technology, audiences*. Don Mills, ON: Oxford University Press.

Gerster, J. (2020, February 28). Racist comments on Indigenous stories prompts outlets to turn them off. *Global News*. https://globalnews.ca/news/6608185/indigenous-wetsuweten-protests/.

Giddens, A. (1984). *The constitution of society: Outline of the theory of structuration*. Cambridge: Polity.

Gillmor, D. (2004). *We the media: Grassroots journalism by the people, for the people*. Sebastopol, CA: O'Reilly.

Gordon, A. (2015). Femsplain: Feminism full-time. Kickstarter. www.kickstarter.com/projects/femsplain/femsplain-feminism-full-time.

Granovetter, M. (1973). The strength of weak ties. *American Journal of Sociology*, 78, 1360–1380.

Grieco, E., Sumida, N., & Fedeli, S. (2018, July 23). About a third of large U.S. newspapers have suffered layoffs since 2017. Pew Research Centre. www.pewresearch.org/fact-tank/2018/07/23/about-a-third-of-large-u-s-newspapers-have-suffered-layoffs-since-2017/.

Griffin, T. (2020, July 16). The Pigeon launches to carve space for new journalists in shrinking media landscape. J-Source. https://j-source.ca/article/the-pigeon-launches-to-carve-space-for-new-journalists-in-shrinking-media-landscape/.

*Guardian* (2009, June 23). MPs' expenses: The Guardian launches major crowdsourcing experiment. www.theguardian.com/gnm-press-office/crowdsourcing-mps-expenses.

Guillory, S. (2019, September 12). The secret to effective business networking. *Forbes*. www.forbes.com/sites/allbusiness/2019/09/21/effective-business-networking-secrets/#67ed57c818a6.

Haas, T. (2005). From "public journalism" to the "public's journalism"? *Journalism Studies*, 6(3), 387–396.

Hassan, R. (2008). *The information society*. Cambridge: Polity Press.

Herman, E., & Chomsky, N. (1988). *Manufacturing consent*. New York: Pantheon Books.

Hermida, A. (2010). Twittering the news: The emergence of ambient journalism. *Journalism Practice*, 4(3), 671–682.

Hermida, A. (2017). Twitter, breaking the news, and hybridity in journalism. In B. Franklin & S. A. Eldridge II (Eds.), *The Routledge companion to digital journalism studies* (pp. 407–426). New York: Routledge.

Hilts, C. [@CraigHilts71] (2020, July 4). *Tornado on the ground south of Glenbain, Saskatchewan, 4:30pm #SKstorm* [*Tweet*]. Twitter. https://twitter.com/Cra ighilts71/status/1279544203563773952.

Hunter, A. (2015). Crowdfunding independent and freelance journalism: Negotiating journalistic norms of autonomy and objectivity. *New Media & Society*, 17(2), 272–288.

Hunter, A. (2016). "It's like having a second full-time job": Crowdfunding, journalism and labour. *Journalism Practice*, 10(2), 217–232.

Hunter, A., & Di Bartolomeo, J. (2018). "We're a movement": Crowdfunding, journalism and feminism. *Feminist Media Studies*, 19(2), 273–287.

Hunter, A., O'Donnell, P., & Cohen, N. (forthcoming). Not "just another job": Journalism as public service. In T. Marjoribanks, L. Zion, P. O'Donnell, & M. Sherwood (Eds.), *Journalists and job loss*. Routledge.

Jian, L., & Shin, J. (2015). Motivations behind donor's contributions to crowdfunded journalism. *Mass Communication and Society*, 18(2), 165–185.

Jian, L., & Usher, N. (2014). Crowd-funded journalism. *Journal of Computer-Mediated Communication*, 19(2), 155–170.

Jirik, J. (2012). Engagement as an emerging norm in international news agency work. In B. St. John III & K. Johnson (Eds.), *News with a view: Essays on the eclipse of objectivity in modern journalism* (pp. 170–186). Jefferson, NC: McFarland & Company.

John, E. (2014, March 13). Veronica Mars, the movie: "Fans gave money, there was all this pressure". *Guardian*. www.theguardian.com/film/2014/mar/13/veronica -mars-movie-fans-money-pressure-return-kickstarter-funded-marshmallows.

Johnson, B. (2012). Matter. Kickstarter. www.kickstarter.com/projects/readma tter/matter.

Jorgenson, D. (2020, August 24). *The @celinedion newsroom @NBCTheVoice parody TikTok you didn't know you needed* [*Tweet*]. Twitter. https://twitter. com/davejorgenson/status/1232033885019607040?lang=en.

Kaplan, R. (2012). The origins of objectivity in American journalism. In S. Allan (Ed.), *The Routledge companion to journalism* (pp. 25–37). London: Routledge.

Kawamoto, K. (2003). Digital journalism: Emerging media and the changing horizons of journalism. In K. Kawamoto (Ed.), *Digital journalism* (pp. 1–29). New York: Rowman & Littlefield.

Kickstarter (n.d.a). Stats. www.kickstarter.com/help/stats.

Kickstarter (n.d.b). Why is funding all-or-nothing. https://help.kickstarter.com/ hc/en-us/articles/115005047893-Why-is-funding-all-or-nothing-.

Kim, Y.-C., & Ball-Rokeach, S. J. (2006). Community storytelling network, neighborhood context, and civic engagement: A multilevel approach. *Human Communication Research*, 32(4), 411–439.

Kleis Nielsen, R. (2015). Introduction: The uncertain future of local journalism. In R. Kleis Nielsen (Ed.), *Local journalism: The decline of newspapers and the rise of digital media* (pp. 1–30). London: I.B. Tauris.

Kliff, S. [@sarahkliff] (2020, February 18). *Totally agree with Ken on this – this kind of proactive outreach is such a useful reporting tool. And it can work to your benefit: when proyou let the world know what you're working on, it puts a stake in the ground* [*Tweet*]. Twitter. https://twitter.com/sarahkliff/status/1229911985954938882.

Knight, W. (2018). Female black journalists and politicians get sent an abusive tweet every 30 seconds. *MIT Technology Review*. www.technologyreview.com/2018/12/18/138551/female-black-journalists-and-politicians-get-sent-an-abusive-tweet-every-30-seconds/.

Kovacevic, K. (2015). Ruby magazine. Kickstarter. www.kickstarter.com/projects/rubythemag/ruby-magazine/description/.

Kuehn, K., & Corrigan, T. F. (2013). Hope labour: The role of employment prospects in online social production. *Political Economy of Communication*, 1(1), 9–25.

Lowery, W. (2020, June 23). A reckoning over objectivity, led by Black journalists. *New York Times*. www.nytimes.com/2020/06/23/opinion/objectivity-black-journalists-coronavirus.html.

Lowrey, W. & Hou, J. (2018). All forest, no trees? Data journalism and the construction of abstract categories. *Journalism*, 1–17. https://doi.org/10.1177/1464884918767577.

Mallick, H. (2017, March 7). *No safe space: Harassment of women in media* [*Video*]. YouTube. www.youtube.com/watch?v=G31rbpbu1ks.

Maras, S. (2013). *Objectivity in journalism*. Cambridge: Polity Press.

McChesney, R. (2004). *The political economy of media*. New York: Monthly Review Press.

McChesney, R., & Pickard, V. (2011). *Will the last reporter please turn out the lights?* New York: New Press.

McDermott, C. (2013, October 2). #ProjectIntern hits the road to capture college intern stories. ProPublica. www.propublica.org/article/projectintern-hits-the-road-to-caputre-college-intern-stories.

Mollick, E. (2014). The dynamics of crowdfunding: An exploratory study. *Journal of Business Venturing*, 29, 1–16.

Mosco, V. (2009). *The political economy of communication*. 2nd ed. London: Sage.

Mustafa, N. (2013). Support my Pakistan and Afghanistan reporting project. Indiegogo. www.indiegogo.com/projects/support-my-pakistan-and-afghanistan-reporting-project#/.

Nel, F. (2010) Laid off: What do UK journalists do next? www.journalism.co.uk/uploads/laidoffreport.pdf.

NPR (n.d.). Lost mothers: Maternal mortality in the U.S. www.npr.org/series/543928389/lost-mothers.

O'Donnell, P., Zion, L., & Sherwood, M. (2016). Where do journalists go after newsroom job cuts? *Journalism Practice*, 10(1), 35–51.

Onuoha, M., Pinder, J., & Schaffer, J. (2015). Guide to crowdsourcing. *Columbia Journalism Review*. www.cjr.org/tow_center_reports/guide_to_crowdsourcing.php/.

Paradis, M., & Poulin-Chartrand, S. (2014). Planète F. Kickstarter. www.kick starter.com/projects/722585604/planete-f.

Pariser, E. (2011). *Filter bubbles.* New York: Penguin.

Parker, J. (2000). *Structuration.* Buckingham: Open University Press.

Parker, L. (2017, May 10). Video game raised $148 million from fans. Now it's raising concerns. *New York Times.* www.nytimes.com/2017/05/10/technolo gy/personaltech/video-game-raised-148-million-from-fans-now-its-raising-is sues.html.

Parris Jr, T. (2017, March 10). Is your member of congress telling it straight on the ACA? Help us fact-check them. ProPublica. www.propublica.org/getin volved/help-us-fact-check-members-of-congress-on-the-affordable-care-act.

Pengelly, M. (2020, June 29). Bob Woodward story on Kavanaugh's veracity "pulled" during Senate hearings. *Guardian.* www.theguardian.com/us-news/ 2020/jun/29/brett-kavanaugh-bob-woodward-washington-post.

Pfauth, E. (2013, November 27). How we turned a world record in journalism crowd-funding into an actual publication. Medium. https://medium.com/ de-correspondent/how-we-turned-a-world-record-in-journalism-crowd-fundin g-into-an-actual-publication-2a06e298afe1.

Pfauth, E. (2015, December 1). Dutch journalism platform De Correspondent reaches milestone of 40,000 paying members. Medium. https://medium.com/ de-correspondent/dutch-journalism-platform-the-correspondent-reaches-miles tone-of-40-000-paying-members-a203251c2de2#.iyljswlui.

*The Pigeon* (n.d.). The Pigeon is creating long-form journalism. Patreon. www. patreon.com/thepigeon.

Porlezza, C., & Splendore, S. (2016). Accountability and transparency of entrepreneurial journalism. *Journalism Practice,* 10(2), 196–216.

Pridmore, J., & Trottier, D. (2014). Extending the audience: Social media marketing, technologies and the construction of markets. In L. McGuigan & V. Manzerolle (Eds.), *The audience commodity in a digital age* (pp. 135–156). New York: Peter Lang.

ProPublica (n.d.). Lost mothers: Maternal care and preventable deaths. www. propublica.org/series/lost-mothers.

PRX (2015). Radiotopia: A storytelling revolution. Kickstarter. www.kicksta rter.com/projects/1748303376/radiotopia-a-storytelling-revolution.

Public Policy Forum (2017). The shattered mirror: News, democracy and trust in the digital age. https://shatteredmirror.ca/.

*Public Record* (n.d.). Our mission as *The Public Record.* www.thepublicrecord. ca/about-the-public-record/.

Puccini, J., Prior, F., & Filali, F. (2018, April 27). How the ABC's biggest crowd-sourced investigation exposed failings in aged care. Australian Broadcasting Corporation. www.abc.net.au/news/about/backstory/investigative-journalism/ 2018-04-27/how-abc-news-crowdsourced-an-aged-care-investigation/9700858.

Raj, A. [@althiaraj] (2020, June 12). *Block. It's the only way to keep sane. I used to mute but now block, block, block. And I report the really offensive things sent to me via DM. Also I deleted the Twitter app* [*Tweet*]. Twitter. https://twitter.com/althiaraj/status/1271313667817000960.

Rosenteil, T. [@TomRosenteil] (2020a, June 24). *I'm not avid on Twitter, but at others' urging I want to offer a thread in response to @wesleylowery's powerful essay in the @nytimes on objectivity, which I liked. But the call for "moral clarity" I believe could use more clarity…Please be patient. This is 1 of 22* [*Tweet*]. Twitter. https://twitter.com/TomRosenstiel/status/1275773988053102592.

Rosenteil, T. [@TomRosenteil] (2020b, June 24). *3… The idea migrated from the sciences to journalism as a sophisticated response to the discovery of unconscious bias in reporting (in particular of Russia)… 3 of 22* [*Tweet*]. Twitter. https://twitter.com/TomRosenstiel/status/1275773989873475589.

Rosenteil, T. [@TomRosenteil] (2020c, June 24). *4… The idea was that journalists needed to employ objective, observable, repeatable methods of verification in their reporting–precisely because they could never be personally objective. Their methods of reporting had to be objective because they never could be… 4 of 22* [*Tweet*]. Twitter. https://twitter.com/TomRosenstiel/status/1275773990729134080.

Rosenteil, T. [@TomRosenteil] (2020d, June 24). *11… Passionate independent inquiry does not mean mindlessly giving both sides equal treatment, thinking there are just two sides to a story, or using balance as an excuse for not doing the work of finding the truth. 11 of 22* [*Tweet*]. Twitter. https://twitter.com/TomRosenstiel/status/1275773996936695809.

Rosenteil, T. [@TomRosenteil] (2020e, June 24). *12…Far from denying personal background, this kind of inquiry recognizes that people's background always enriches their journalism, be it WASP or Buddhist, White, Black, Jew, Latina or Latino, male or female. This is the way to recognize bias and avoid unconscious slant…* [*Tweet*]. Twitter. https://twitter.com/TomRosenstiel/status/1275773997758767105.

Rosenteil, T. [@TomRosenteil] (2020f, June 24). *18… If journalists replace a flawed understanding of objectivity by taking refuge in subjectivity and think their opinions have more moral integrity than genuine inquiry, journalism will be lost. 18 of 22* [*Tweet*]. Twitter. https://twitter.com/TomRosenstiel/status/1275774002796072960.

Schudson, M. (2001). The objectivity norm in American journalism. *Journalism*, 2(2), 149–170.

Schudson, M., & Anderson, C. (2009). Objectivity, professionalism and truth seeking in journalism. In K. Wahl-Jorgensen & T. Hanitzsch (Eds.), *Handbook of journalism studies* (pp. 88–101). New York: Routledge.

Schwienbacher, A., & Larralde, B. (2012). Crowdfunding of small entrepreneurial ventures. In D. Cumming (Ed.), *The Oxford handbook of entrepreneurial finance* (pp. 369–391). New York: Oxford University Press.

Seabrook, A. (2013). DecodeDC. Kickstarter. www.kickstarter.com/projects/1832422021/decodedc.

Silverman, C. (2020, March 23). The coronavirus is a media extinction event. BuzzFeed News. www.buzzfeednews.com/article/craigsilverman/coronavirus-news-industry-layoffs.

Simon, M. (2010, January 13). What we're hearing via social media. CNN. www.cnn.com/2010/TECH/01/13/haiti.social.media/index.html.

Simpson, K. [@CBCKatie] (2020, June 12). *I dread looking at my phone due to high volume of angry content that is typically not related to my journalism. Open to suggestions on ways to reduce receiving such content, and ways to support other journalists going through same* [*Tweet*]. Twitter. https://twitter.com/CBCKatie/status/1271294251264086016.

Singer, J. B. (2015). Out of bounds: Professional norms as boundary markers. In M. Carlson & S. C. Lewis (Eds.), *Boundaries of journalism: Professionalism, practice and participation* (pp. 21–36). London: Routledge.

Smith, J. (2016, December 20). We're getting rid of comments on VICE.com but that doesn't mean we don't love you. Vice. www.vice.com/en_us/article/vvdjjy/were-getting-rid-of-comments-on-vice.

Smythe, D. (1981). *Dependency road*. New York: Ablex.

St. John III, B., & Johnson, K. (2012). Introduction: Challenges for journalism in a post-objective age. In B. St. John III & K. Johnson (Eds.), *News with a view: Essays on the eclipse of objectivity in modern journalism* (pp. 1–8). Jefferson, NC: McFarland & Company.

Stephens, M. (2007). *A history of news*. New York: Oxford University Press.

Sunstein, C. (2007). *Republic.com 2.0*. Princeton, NJ: Princeton University Press.

*Texas Tribune* (n.d.). Code of ethics. www.texastribune.org/about/ethics/.

Thomas, R. (2013). The Veronica Mars movie project. Kickstarter. www.kickstarter.com/projects/559914737/the-veronica-mars-movie-project.

Thompson, C. (2008). Brave new world of digital intimacy. *New York Times*. www.nytimes.com/2008/09/07/magazine/07awareness-t.html.

Tobin, A., Gallardo, A., Jaffe, L., & Raghavendran, B. (2019, January 15). What engagement reporting does—and doesn't—mean at ProPublica. ProPublica. www.propublica.org/article/what-does-engagement-reporting-mean-propublica.

Trasel, M., & Fontoura, M. (2015). Crowdfunding and pluralisation: Comparison between the coverage of the participatory website Spot.Us and the American press. In L. Bennett, B. Chin, & B. Jones (Eds.), *Crowdfunding the future* (pp. 99–115). New York: Peter Lang.

Tuchman, G. (1972). Objectivity as strategic ritual: An examination of newsmen's notions of objectivity. *American Journal of Sociology*, 77(4), 660–679.

*Tyee* (n.d.). What is The Tyee? https://thetyee.ca/About/Us/.

Viererbl, B., & Koch, T. (2019). Once a journalist, not always a journalist? Causes and consequences of job changes from journalism to public relations. *Journalism*, 1–17. https://doi.org/10.1177/1464884919829647.

Vogt, N., & Mitchell, A. (2016). Crowdfunded journalism: A small but growing addition to publicly funded journalism. Pew Research Centre. www.journalism.org/2016/01/20/crowdfunded-journalism/.

WBEZ (n.d.). Curious city. www.wbez.org/shows/curious-city/7b79e16d-f3a9-4156-9b27-4d2cc6ce351e.

Westcott, L. (2019). Why newsrooms need a solution to end online harassment of reporters. Committee to Protect Journalists. https://cpj.org/2019/09/news rooms-solution-online-harassment-canada-usa/.

Winston, B., & Winston, M. (2021). *The roots of fake news: Objecting to objective journalism.* London: Routledge.

Zara, C. (2013, January 10). The year of Kickstarter journalism: Crowdfunding is doing what the news industry can't. *International Business Times.* www.ibtimes.com/year-kickstarter-journalism-crowdfunding-doing-what-news-industry-cant -1007836.

# Index

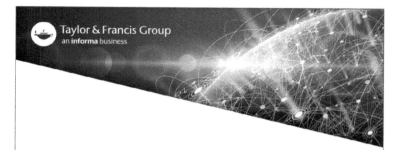

www.ingramcontent.com/pod-product-compliance
Ingram Content Group UK Ltd.
Pitfield, Milton Keynes, MK11 3LW, UK
UKHW020424010325
455677UK00029B/989